ANDREA LEVY

Andrea Levy was born in London in 1956 to Jamaican parents who came to Britain in 1948; her father sailed from Jamaica to England on the *Empire Windrush* ship and her mother joined him soon after.

After attending writing workshops in her mid-thirties, Andrea Levy began to write the novels that she, as a young woman, had always wanted to read; novels that reflect the experiences of black Britons, which look at Britain and its changing populations and at the intimacies that bind British history with that of the Caribbean.

Andrea Levy wrote five novels and was a recipient of an Arts Council Award. Her second novel *Never Far from Nowhere* was long-listed for the Orange Prize while *Small Island* was the winner of the Orange Prize for Fiction, the Whitbread Novel Award, the Whitbread Book of the Year Award, the Orange Best of the Best, and the Commonwealth Writer's Prize. Her last novel *The Long Song* was shortlisted for the Man Booker Prize, and was the winner of the Walter Scott Prize for Historical Fiction. Besides novels, Andrea Levy wrote short stories that have been read on radio, published in newspapers and anthologised.

HELEN EDMUNDSON

Helen Edmundson's first play, *Flying*, was presented at the National Theatre Studio in 1990. In 1992, she adapted Tolstoy's *Anna Karenina* for Shared Experience, for whom she also adapted *The Mill on the Floss* in 1994. Both won awards – the TMA and the Time Out Awards respectively – and both productions were twice revived and extensively toured. Shared Experience also staged her original adaptation of *War and Peace* at the National Theatre in 1996, and toured her adaptations of Mary Webb's *Gone to Earth* in 2004, Euripides' *Orestes* in 2006, the new two-part version of *War and Peace* in 2008, and the original play *Mary Shelley* in 2012. Her original play *The Clearing* was first staged at the Bush Theatre in 1993, winning the John Whiting and Time Out Awards, *Mother Teresa is Dead* was premiered at the Royal Court Theatre in 2002, *The Heresy of Love* was premiered by the Royal Shakespeare Company in the Swan Theatre in 2012, and revived at Shakespeare's Globe in 2015, and *Queen Anne* was premiered by the Royal Shakespeare Company in the Swan Theatre in 2015, and revived at the Theatre Royal Haymarket in 2017. Her adaptation of Jamila Gavin's *Coram Boy* premiered at the National Theatre to critical acclaim in 2005, receiving a Time Out Award. It was subsequently revived in 2006, and produced on Broadway in 2007. She adapted Calderón's *Life is a Dream* for the Donmar Warehouse in 2009, and Arthur Ransome's *Swallows and Amazons* for the Bristol Old Vic in 2010, which subsequently transferred to the West End before embarking on a national tour in 2012. Her adaptation of *Thérèse Raquin* premiered at the Theatre Royal Bath in 2014, and was subsequently produced on Broadway by Roundabout Theatre Company in 2015. Helen was awarded a Windham Campbell Literature Prize by Yale University in 2015.

Andrea Levy

SMALL ISLAND

adapted for the stage by
Helen Edmundson

NICK HERN BOOKS
London
www.nickhernbooks.co.uk

A Nick Hern Book

This adaptation of *Small Island* first published in Great Britain as a paperback original in 2019 by Nick Hern Books Limited, The Glasshouse, 49a Goldhawk Road, London

Small Island (play) copyright © 2019 Helen Edmundson
Small Island (book) copyright © 2004 Andrea Levy, published by Headline Review

Cover image by Franklyn Rodgers

Designed and typeset by Nick Hern Books, London
Printed in the UK by Mimeo Ltd, Huntingdon, Cambridgeshire PE29 6XX

A CIP catalogue record for this book is available from the British Library

ISBN 978 1 84842 851 5

Small Island was first performed in the Olivier auditorium of the National Theatre, London, on 1 May 2019 (previews from 17 April). The cast, in order of speaking, was as follows:

MRS RYDER	Amy Forrest
HORTENSE	Leah Harvey
MISS JEWEL	Sandra James-Young
LITTLE HORTENSE	Keira Chansa, Aiko Foueillis-Mosé, Nova Foueillis-Mosé
MR PHILIP/G.I./KENNETH	Trevor Laird
MISS MA	Jacqueline Boatswain
LITTLE MICHAEL	Shaquahn Crowe, Raphael Higgins-Humes, Quincy Miller-Cole
MICHAEL	CJ Beckford
POLICEMAN/G.I.	Natey Jones
WOMAN IN HURRICANE	Chereen Buckley
BERNARD	Andrew Rothney
QUEENIE	Aisling Loftus
AUNT DOROTHY/ WOMAN WITH BABY	Beatie Edney
MRS BUXTON/MISS TODD/ WOMAN/WOMAN IN CINEMA	Stephanie Jacob
MR BUXTON/GINGER/ SERGEANT THWAITES/ RAILWAY WORKER	Adam Ewan
YOUNG MAN IN SWEETSHOP/ KIP/G.I./RAILWAY WORKER	Cavan Clarke
ARTHUR	David Fielder
FRANNY	Phoebe Frances Brown, Rebecca Lee
GILBERT	Gershwyn Eustache Jnr
RECRUITING OFFICER ONE/ SOAMES/RAILWAY WORKER/ MILITARY POLICEMAN	Paul Bentall

ELWOOD	Johann Myers
RECRUITING OFFICER TWO/	John Hastings
G.I./FOREMAN	
USHERETTE	CJ Johnson
G.I.	Daniel Norford
CELIA	Shiloh Coke

Other parts played by members of the company

UNDERSTUDIES

ARTHUR	Paul Bentall
HORTENSE/MISS MA	Chereen Buckley
MISS JEWEL/WOMAN	Shiloh Coke
MANAGER/MAN/KIP	Adam Ewan
BERNARD	John Hastings
GILBERT	Natey Jones
QUEENIE	Rebecca Lee
MR PHILIP/KENNETH	Johann Myers
MICHAEL/ELWOOD	Daniel Norford

SUPERNUMERARIES

Jamie Ankrah, Aimee Louise Bevan, Thea Day, Victoria Denard,
Alma Eno, Alvin Ikenwe, Luther King Osei, Alice Langrish,
Roberta Livingston, Fatima Niemogha, Anselm Onyenani,
Mary Tillett, Joseph Vaiana, Tricia Wey, Christopher Williams,
Joylon Young

ON FILM

Alyn Hawke and Gemma Sutton

Music recorded by	Jazz Jamaica All Stars
Additional music recorded by	London String Group

Director	Rufus Norris
Set and Costume Designer	Katrina Lindsay
Projection Designer	Jon Driscoll
Lighting Designer	Paul Anderson
Composer and Rehearsal Music Director	Benjamin Kwasi Burrell
Sound Designer	Ian Dickinson
Movement Director	Coral Messam
Fight Director	Kate Waters
Music Supervisor	Marc Tritschler
Music Consultant	Gary Crosby
Company Voice Work	Jeannette Nelson
Dialect Coach	Hazel Holder
Associate Set and Costume Designer	Sadeysa Greenaway-Bailey
Associate Projection Designer	Gino Ricardo Green
Staff Director	Anna Himali Howard
Associate Music Director	Shiloh Coke

Characters

HORTENSE
MRS RYDER
LITTLE HORTENSE
MISS JEWEL
MR PHILIP
MISS MA
LITTLE MICHAEL
MICHAEL
POLICEMAN
WOMAN IN HURRICANE
BERNARD
QUEENIE
AUNT DOROTHY
MR BUXTON
MRS BUXTON
YOUNG MAN
ARTHUR
FRANNY
KIP
GINGER
GILBERT
WHITE G.I.
OFFICER 1

OFFICER 2
ELWOOD
FLIGHT SERGEANT
    THWAITES
WOMAN WITH BABY
G.I. 1
G.I. 2
USHERETTE
WHITE G.I. 2
CINEMA MANAGER
AMERICAN MILITARY
    POLICEMAN
CELIA LANGLEY
CAPTAIN SOAMES
KENNETH
MISS TODD
FOREMAN
WORKER 1
WORKER 2
WORKER 3

And REPORTERS, LOCALS, VOLUNTEERS, ASSISTANT,
OLD LADY, WHITE G.I.s, BLACK G.I.s, WEST INDIAN
RECRUITS, AMERICAN MILITARY POLICEMEN,
EX-SERVICEMEN, MEN, WOMEN

*This text went to press before the end of rehearsals and so may
differ slightly from the play as performed.*

ACT ONE

Scene One

Summer. 1939.

Pathé-style news footage of Jamaica bracing itself for a strong hurricane.

On the stage, in a wooden schoolhouse, HORTENSE *is hurrying to prepare the classroom for the hurricane's arrival.* MRS RYDER *is standing by the open doorway. Strong gusts of wind are heard.*

MRS RYDER. Why, listen to that wind, Hortense! I do believe it's on its way.

HORTENSE. Yes, Mrs Ryder. It is certainly drawing closer now.

MRS RYDER. Oh, look how the trees are starting to sway! Why, it's as if they're dancing!

HORTENSE. Yes, Mrs Ryder.

MRS RYDER. My very first hurricane. How thrilling! Oh!

HORTENSE *pauses in what she's doing and looks at the audience. She addresses them, conspiratorially, with barely controlled excitement.*

HORTENSE (*to audience*). I think, perchance, that you are wondering how I come to find myself in this schoolhouse with this fool-fool American woman who believe a hurricane on the island of Jamaica is something to look forward to.

MRS RYDER. Oh, my! I do believe it's almost here!

HORTENSE (*to audience*). I must confess that I feel just a little bit sorry for this lady – Mrs Ryder, evangelist, schoolteacher. She clearly believe that *she* is the heroine of this situation, but I can assure you, *she* is most certainly not.

MRS RYDER. Let's leave the door unlocked, shall we? In case someone wants to join us.

HORTENSE. Like Mr Ryder.

MRS RYDER. Yes, Hortense. Exactly. Like Mr Ryder.

Now, where's my purse? I think this calls for lipstick!

MRS RYDER *locates her handbag, takes out her lipstick and puts some on.*

HORTENSE (*to audience*). The reason I am in this schoolhouse is that I choose to be. I am only a classroom assistant after all and, like the pupils, I could have left at lunchtime when word of the approaching storm was verified. But to do such a sensible thing would be to deny the man I love the opportunity to come and rescue me. For him to say, 'Hortense! But where is Hortense?! Perhaps she's in the schoolhouse, perhaps she is alone, afraid! I must risk my life and run to her at once!'

MRS RYDER. I swear the Lord is present in that wind. Oh, come, wind, for I am ready!

HORTENSE (*to audience*). I will tell you the story of my love. It is a love with deep-down roots.

Enter HORTENSE *as a little child, skipping and playing on a wooded path. Enter* MISS JEWEL *behind her.*

MISS JEWEL. Hortense! Hortense! Come-come, me sprigadee.

LITTLE HORTENSE. How much further to the big house with the chickens?

MISS JEWEL. Not much further nah.

LITTLE HORTENSE. Miss Jewel, if I no like the big house with the chickens, can we go back to Mama?

MISS JEWEL. Nuh, I tell yah – your mama gone work in another country nah. She far, far away. In Cuba.

LITTLE HORTENSE. But what if she come back to look for us?

MISS JEWEL. She know we gone to your papa folk.

LITTLE HORTENSE. Who is my papa? (*Receiving no reply.*) Miss Jewel? Grandmama?

MISS JEWEL. Your papa him big-big man. Important man.

LITTLE HORTENSE. At the big house?

MISS JEWEL. Him government man. Him far, far away. In Kingston.

LITTLE HORTENSE *suddenly stops.*

LITTLE HORTENSE. Miss Jewel, I no want to go to the big house with the chickens.

MISS JEWEL *stops and looks at her. She crouches down and beckons to* LITTLE HORTENSE –

MISS JEWEL. Come.

LITTLE HORTENSE *goes to her.* MISS JEWEL *takes hold of one of* LITTLE HORTENSE*'s arms.*

This your papa's skin.

LITTLE HORTENSE. My skin is the colour of warm honey.

MISS JEWEL. You a lucky, lucky chile. This skin is a golden life. You wa golden life, me sprigadee?

LITTLE HORTENSE (*enchanted*). Oh, yes. I wa golden life.

MISS JEWEL. So shift yuh battam nah.

They walk on. Then MISS JEWEL *stops.*

This the place.

HORTENSE (*to audience*). A long track. A white house nestled amongst palm trees. The biggest house I've ever seen. Made of stone, with tiles upon the roof.

Enter MR PHILIP, MISS MA *and* LITTLE MICHAEL. LITTLE MICHAEL *hangs back, watching.*

MR PHILIP. So this is Lovell's child.

MISS JEWEL. Yessir. This Hortense, sir.

MR PHILIP. Hum. (*To* LITTLE HORTENSE.) I am your father's cousin, Mr Philip Roberts. You may call me Mr Philip. This is my wife, Mrs Martha Roberts. You are a fortunate child. Your father wishes you to be raised in a decent home and to have some teaching. So from now on you will live with us.

LITTLE HORTENSE *is too frightened to speak.*

This is a God-fearing house. I hope you are acquainted with the Lord?

LITTLE HORTENSE *looks at* MISS JEWEL *doubtfully.*

MISS JEWEL. Oh, yessir. The Lord him very good man, sir.

MR PHILIP. Hum.

MR PHILIP *walks away into the house.*

MISS MA. Michael, don't be shy now. Come and meet your cousin.

LITTLE MICHAEL *approaches, grinning. His hands are clasped behind his back.*

Hortense, this is our son, Michael.

LITTLE HORTENSE (*quietly*). Hello.

LITTLE MICHAEL. Hello.

He holds out his hand towards her. In his hand there is a small gecko. LITTLE HORTENSE *just looks at it.*

MISS MA. Oh! Oh, put it down, Michael. You are a mischievous boy.

LITTLE MICHAEL (*to* LITTLE HORTENSE). Why don't you jump?

LITTLE HORTENSE. Because it is a gecko. I like geckos.

MISS MA (*to* MICHAEL). Take Hortense to her bedroom now.

Miss Jewel, I will show you where you sleep.

LITTLE HORTENSE. But… I sleep with my grandmama.

MISS MA. No. Miss Jewel will sleep in the wash house.

LITTLE HORTENSE. But…

MISS JEWEL. Nuh fret nah, me sprigadee…

MISS MA. And there will be no more of that talk. This is Miss Hortense. And this is Master Michael.

MISS MA *leads* MISS JEWEL *away towards the wash house*. LITTLE MICHAEL *runs towards the gardens at the back of the house*.

LITTLE MICHAEL (*to* LITTLE HORTENSE). Come on! Come!

LITTLE HORTENSE *runs after him. They arrive at a large tree. There's a rickety table in front of it*.

LITTLE HORTENSE. She tell you to show me where I will sleep.

LITTLE MICHAEL (*pointing to a hollow in the tree*). Look. You see that hole in the tree? There is a woodpecker's nest in that hole. There must be – I've seen them coming and going. (*Indicating the table*.) Climb on there and bend over.

LITTLE HORTENSE. What?

LITTLE MICHAEL. I need to climb on your back.

LITTLE HORTENSE *climbs on the table and bends over*. LITTLE MICHAEL *climbs onto the table and then stands on her back. He can just see into the hole*.

Yes! I can see it! Keep still.

He stretches up and reaches into the hole.

LITTLE HORTENSE. What are you doing?

LITTLE MICHAEL. I just need to… I'm trying to reach an egg.

LITTLE HORTENSE. No!

She moves to stand up. LITTLE MICHAEL *is forced to step off her back quickly. He falls off the table and lands on the ground. He lies still*.

(*Horrified*.) Michael? Michael?

He suddenly sits up and rubs his head in a comical way. She laughs nervously. He jumps to his feet. She chases him. They laugh.

I'm sorry about your head.

LITTLE MICHAEL. I forgive you. But I will get you back for it.

LITTLE HORTENSE. How?

LITTLE MICHAEL. It will be a surprise. I will show you the best tree to climb. We have many, many trees. Come on.

They start to run off but LITTLE MICHAEL *stops.*

You must tell my father about everything you do today.

LITTLE HORTENSE. All right.

LITTLE MICHAEL. Tell him at suppertime. He will like that very much.

That evening. The dinner table. MR PHILIP, MISS MA, LITTLE MICHAEL *and* LITTLE HORTENSE *are seated at the table.* MISS JEWEL *is standing close by, waiting to serve. All have their hands together and their heads bowed.*

MR PHILIP. God is great and God is good, and we thank Him for this food. By His hand we all are fed. Give us Lord our daily bread. Through Christ our Lord, Amen.

MISS MA/MICHAEL. Amen.

LITTLE HORTENSE (*quietly*). Amen.

MISS JEWEL (*loudly*). Amen-Amen!

MISS JEWEL moves to serve, but MR PHILIP *suddenly stands, clutching his Bible.*

MR PHILIP. 'I am the way, the truth and the life. No man cometh unto the Father but by me. If ye had known me, ye should have known my father also: and from henceforth ye have known him and have seen God.'

MR PHILIP *sits.*

MISS MA (*to* MISS JEWEL). You may serve.

MR PHILIP. Water first.

MISS JEWEL takes up the water jug and begins to fill MR PHILIP's *glass. Silently,* LITTLE MICHAEL *prompts* LITTLE HORTENSE *to speak.*

LITTLE HORTENSE. I have a lot of fun today.

MISS MA. No speaking at the table, child.

LITTLE HORTENSE *glances at* LITTLE MICHAEL, *who kicks her under the table in encouragement.*

LITTLE HORTENSE. But Mr Philip will want to know. I have been looking at a woodpecker's nest and I have been climbing trees.

MISS MA. No speaking!

MR PHILIP. Wait. You have been doing what?

LITTLE HORTENSE. Climbing trees. I climbed the tree with the branches that go out across the water and...

MR PHILIP. What ungodliness is this? You think it is godly to lift yourself into the branches of a tree like a monkey?

LITTLE HORTENSE. I...

MR PHILIP. Little girls do not climb trees. Principle! Each one of us will stand accountable, puny and small, in front of the Almighty. You will learn principle! Get out of my sight.

Shaking with fear, LITTLE HORTENSE *stands.*

MISS JEWEL. But she nuh have her...

MISS MA. Be quiet! (*To* LITTLE HORTENSE.) Leave the table. You will have no supper.

LITTLE HORTENSE *glances at* LITTLE MICHAEL. *He is looking down. She leaves.*

(*To* MISS JEWEL.) You may serve.

The sun has set. LITTLE HORTENSE *is sitting in the chicken shed.* LITTLE MICHAEL *approaches.*

LITTLE MICHAEL (*quietly*). Hortense! Hortense!

LITTLE HORTENSE. Go away.

LITTLE MICHAEL. What are you doing in the chicken shed?

LITTLE HORTENSE. Don't try to come in. There isn't room.

LITTLE MICHAEL (*coming in*). Move up.

He squashes in beside her. He takes a piece of chicken from his pocket, wrapped in a napkin, and holds it out to her.

I brought you this.

LITTLE HORTENSE. I don't want it.

He shrugs and is about to put it away but she takes it and eats it hungrily.

LITTLE MICHAEL (*smirking*). You're eating chicken in a chicken shed.

She gives him a look and carries on.

(*Pointing.*) That hen's laying an egg.

LITTLE HORTENSE. I know.

LITTLE MICHAEL. Why wouldn't you let me take the woodpecker's egg?

LITTLE HORTENSE. Because when you take things away from their mothers they die.

LITTLE MICHAEL. You're taken away from your mother but you're not dead.

LITTLE HORTENSE *begins to cry.*

Do you like night-fishing? We'll go to the stream. We'll make rods from branches.

She doesn't respond.

I'm sorry about your supper.

LITTLE HORTENSE. I forgive you. But I will get you back for it.

LITTLE MICHAEL (*excited*). How?

LITTLE HORTENSE. It will be a surprise.

HORTENSE (*to audience*). All my days when I was small were filled with Michael Roberts. He was allowed to play all day but I had chores to do. I had to help Miss Jewel in the wash house, I had to clean the kerosene lamps and keep the area around the tamarind tree free from dirt and a pleasure to sit in. But Michael was always –

LITTLE MICHAEL. Come now, Hortense. Leave all that. Come now!

HORTENSE. And we would run away into the fields to fill our tummies with star apples and raspberries and mangoes, or chase the goats around the yard and ride them like horses.

Some years later. Outside the house, MR PHILIP, MISS MA *and* LITTLE MICHAEL *are waiting.* LITTLE MICHAEL *is dressed in a smart jacket and has a small suitcase.*

MR PHILIP (*to* LITTLE MICHAEL). It is time to surrender the deeds of thy younger years and to walk in the way of God as a man.

HORTENSE (*to audience*). The day Michael left to attend boarding school in the city, I squeezed my nails into my hand until blood pricked on my skin, because I didn't want to cry.

MISS MA (*straightening* LITTLE MICHAEL*'s tie*). Your tie is not straight. Don't forget to keep your ears clean. Oh, my boy. Say goodbye to your papa now.

LITTLE MICHAEL *goes to stand in front of* MR PHILIP, *who suddenly embraces him.*

MR PHILIP. You will make me proud, son.

LITTLE MICHAEL (*clinging to his father*). Yes, I will, Papa.

MR PHILIP. The time will pass quickly.

There is the sound of a van approaching.

MISS MA. The van is coming! I hear it! I hear it!

MISS MA *rushes to meet the van.* MR PHILIP, *for fear of being overcome, withdraws.* LITTLE HORTENSE *approaches* LITTLE MICHAEL.

LITTLE HORTENSE. Michael?

LITTLE MICHAEL. I am going to the best school in the whole world, Hortense. And you will be staying at the penny-a-week government school, skipping silly rhymes and doing baby sums.

LITTLE HORTENSE. No, I won't.

LITTLE MICHAEL. And counting frogs at the base of the tree.

LITTLE HORTENSE. No, I won't!

LITTLE MICHAEL. I feel sorry for you.

LITTLE HORTENSE (*furious*). Sorry for me? No one needs to feel sorry for me!

MISS MA (*calling*). Michael!

LITTLE HORTENSE. Go then.

MISS MA. Michael, come now!

LITTLE MICHAEL. Sorry.

She doesn't reply.

I said sorry.

He starts to leave.

LITTLE HORTENSE. I forgive you. But I will get you back for it.

He grins at her. He leaves. LITTLE HORTENSE *hears the sound of the van's engine. She listens as it drives away.*

HORTENSE (*to audience*). He came home only three times and each time his head was bigger. The last time, his voice was strange and he didn't want to talk to me or to look for the woodpecker's nest. But then, six weeks ago, Michael Roberts finished school and came back home for good. And he was...

Enter MICHAEL, *eighteen years old. A well-cut suit, a white shirt, a tie held in place by a pin. A hat tipped at an angle, a thin moustache, a mischievous smile.* MR PHILIP, MISS MA, MISS JEWEL *and* HORTENSE *form a welcoming committee.*

MISS MA. Michael? Look at you, son! I send a boy to boarding school and see what they send me back – a man!

MICHAEL. Hello, Mama. (*Going to* MR PHILIP *and shaking his hand.*) Papa.

MR PHILIP *looks disturbed by this new* MICHAEL, *but is pleased to see him nonetheless.*

MR PHILIP. Welcome home, Michael.

MICHAEL (*looking at* HORTENSE). And who is this?

HORTENSE. You know who I am, Michael Roberts.

MICHAEL (*looking her up and down*). My, but Miss Hortense
– you are all grown up.

HORTENSE *makes a strange, giggling, nervous noise.*
MICHAEL *turns his gaze on* MISS JEWEL.

Miss Jewel. (*Nodding slowly.*) Miss Jewel.

He suddenly rushes to MISS JEWEL, *picks her up and spins
her around. She shrieks and laughs.*

Miss Jewel! Oh, boy, how I miss you spice-up chicken!

MISS MA *looks nervously at* MR PHILIP, *whose face is set
in an expression of amazement and concern.*

MISS MA, MICHAEL *and* HORTENSE *are seated at the
table.* MISS JEWEL *is waiting to serve.* MICHAEL *looks
across at* HORTENSE *and smiles so sweetly that she blushes
and can hardly breathe.* MR PHILIP *is standing at the head
of the table, reading from his Bible.*

MR PHILIP. 'And God said, "Let there be Light", and there
was light. And God saw that the light was good, and God
separated the light from the darkness. God called the light
Day, and the darkness, He called Night.'

MR PHILIP *closes his Bible and sits.*

MICHAEL. This is very interesting, Papa. But I have been
taught at school that the earth moves around the sun, and that
it is this movement which causes...

MISS MA (*shocked*). Michael. It is rude to speak at the table.

MR PHILIP *is staring at* MICHAEL. HORTENSE *is
watching, wide-eyed.*

MICHAEL. Oh, Mama. I am a grown man now. And I can
assure you that it is quite normal to discuss things at the
table. Tell me, Papa, what do you think of the notion that
men are descended from monkeys?

MISS MA. Michael!

MR PHILIP. Are you questioning the Lord thy God? Are you presuming to question the teachings of thy maker, the Almighty, the King of Kings?

MICHAEL. No, Papa. But I believe it is a popular scientific opinion that men are descended from apes. Have you heard of Mr Darwin, Papa?

MR PHILIP (*slamming his Bible on the table*). Enough! There will be no blasphemy in this house!

HORTENSE suddenly giggles with anxiety and shock. MISS MA hits her across the face. In the silence that follows, MISS JEWEL sucks her teeth. MICHAEL stares at MR PHILIP, undaunted.

Get out.

MICHAEL. I am asking for a civilised discussion.

MR PHILIP. Get out!

MICHAEL. No.

Silence.

MR PHILIP (*to MISS MA and HORTENSE*). Come. (*Seeing them hesitate.*) Come!

MISS MA *and* HORTENSE *stand.*

We will not eat with a blasphemer. There will be no blasphemy in *my* house!

MISS MA *and* HORTENSE *follow* MR PHILIP *out.* MISS JEWEL *goes after them.*

Later. HORTENSE *is on the veranda cleaning the kerosene lamps.* MICHAEL *comes out and watches her. She sees him and smiles, shyly.*

MICHAEL. Still cleaning the lamps?

HORTENSE. Yes.

He takes out a cigarette. He sees her watching. He offers her one. She hesitates.

MICHAEL. There's always a first time.

HORTENSE. No. I...

MICHAEL (*lighting his cigarette*). I'm sorry about your face.

HORTENSE. I forgive you.

He smiles.

MICHAEL. Let me see.

(*Touching her cheek.*) No harm done.

I like the dress.

HORTENSE. Oh. Mrs Ryder gave it to me. It's one she has finished with.

MICHAEL. Mrs Ryder?

HORTENSE. The schoolteacher. I am working at a church school. Only as an assistant but...

MICHAEL. That's good.

HORTENSE. Yes. I had to take the dress in a little because Mrs Ryder is more... We are very different shapes.

MICHAEL (*nodding*). And is there a Mr Ryder?

HORTENSE. Oh, yes. But... But he is not as good as he ought to be. You will see him driving around in his big American car going places he should not go.

MICHAEL. Is that right?

HORTENSE. No one can understand it because Mrs Ryder is still quite a pretty lady. She has blonde hair and pale, pale skin. All the men are saying it is a crime that she is left to walk around the town unescorted. I don't know why I'm telling you all this.

MICHAEL. We're making conversation. There's not enough conversation in this house.

So, Hortense, are we going to look for the woodpecker?

HORTENSE (*smiling*). If you want to.

MICHAEL. Sure I want to.

He walks over to the tree. She goes towards him but then hesitates.

HORTENSE. You aren't going to climb on my back?

MICHAEL. Well, I don't know. You will have to trust me.

He holds out his hand to her and she goes to him. He grabs her and lifts her above his head.

HORTENSE. Ah!

She looks into the hole.

Three eggs! It is a fine sight.

MICHAEL. Not as fine as the sight from down here.

HORTENSE. Oh!

He puts her down, laughing. She straightens her skirt.

Michael Roberts. You are a very mischievous… man.

HORTENSE *takes a moment to recover her composure.*

(*To audience.*) These last few weeks he has barely left my side. Why, two weeks ago I found him outside this schoolhouse –

MICHAEL *is talking to* MRS RYDER *outside the schoolhouse.* HORTENSE *comes out.* MICHAEL *and* MRS RYDER *move apart quickly.*

Michael. What are you doing here?

MICHAEL. I've come to escort you home. What else?

HORTENSE. I am perfectly capable of walking home alone.

Mrs Ryder, this is my cousin, Michael Roberts.

MICHAEL. Mrs Ryder and I are already acquainted.

HORTENSE. Are you?

MRS RYDER (*flustered*). Yes. Of course. We… we met in church…

HORTENSE. In church? Oh, Michael does not go to church. You must be mistaken.

MRS RYDER. Oh. Yes…

MICHAEL (*mischievously*). Now where could we have met, Mrs Ryder?

MRS RYDER (*blushing*). I... Well, I...

MICHAEL (*holding out his arm*). You ready, Hortense?

HORTENSE (*taking his arm*). Michael is always worrying about me.

MRS RYDER. How sweet.

MICHAEL. Good day, Mrs Ryder.

MRS RYDER. Good day.

HORTENSE and MICHAEL begin to walk away, but then HORTENSE stops. She watches MICHAEL as he leaves. She sighs with happiness.

HORTENSE (*to audience*). Yesterday we walked through the town together and I heard someone murmur, 'What a fine young couple.' I almost fainted with pride. So you see, tonight I am certain that he will come for me. And if he does, when he does, I will know that our destiny is sealed.

We are back where we began, only now the hurricane has arrived. In the schoolhouse, MRS RYDER is now cowering as the terrible winds howl and tear around the building. There is a terrific crash as a tree comes down close by. MRS RYDER screams.

MRS RYDER. Aah!

HORTENSE (*rushing to her*). Mrs Ryder, you must try to keep calm now.

MRS RYDER. What's happening? This can't be right. Oh, my Lord. My Lord...

HORTENSE. Please. You must try to breathe.

MRS RYDER. Oh, where is he? I want him. I want him!

HORTENSE. I'm sure Mr Ryder is safe. Wherever he happens to be. I'm sure he will take shelter.

There is another huge howl. It seems as if the roof will blow off. MRS RYDER screams hysterically.

Mrs Ryder. Please. This will not help.

Suddenly, there is a banging on the schoolhouse door.
MICHAEL*'s voice is heard.*

MICHAEL (*off*). Hello?! Hello?!

HORTENSE. Michael. (*To audience*.) He is here! Oh, he has come!

She rushes to the door, leaving MRS RYDER *shrieking and sobbing. She pulls open the door as –*

Michael.

MICHAEL *rushes in. He is breathing hard from running. He stands for a moment, wiping rain from his eyes, his shirt is soaked and clinging to him.*

Michael Roberts. I am perfectly capable of surviving a hurricane. You should not have…

But MICHAEL*'s eyes are not on her. Moving* HORTENSE *out of the way, he rushes to* MRS RYDER.

MICHAEL. Stella.

MRS RYDER. Michael…

MICHAEL. Stella. It's all right. It's all right. I'm here now. Stella. Stella.

HORTENSE. 'Stella'?

There is another crash. MRS RYDER *screams –*

MRS RYDER. Oh, make it stop!

He takes MRS RYDER *is his arms and kisses her passionately.* HORTENSE *is staring at them, transfixed.*

MICHAEL. Oh, Stella.

HORTENSE (*quietly*). No.

HORTENSE *suddenly turns and runs from the schoolhouse. She is out in the raging hurricane, and the ferocious, howling winds are matched by the wild intensity of her rage and pain.*

As the wind begins to subside, HORTENSE *stands, panting for breath and shaking. The rain comes down heavily now. She runs and suddenly stops. Ahead of her is a small crowd of people. She moves closer. Through the rain she can see a* POLICEMAN *who is trying to keep the crowd back.*

POLICEMAN. Road closed! Find another way round!

People are straining their necks to see something. HORTENSE *reaches the back of the crowd. A* WOMAN *turns from the crowd and walks back past* HORTENSE, *shaking her head.*

HORTENSE. What's happened?

WOMAN. Car gone into a tree. What an awful sight.

HORTENSE. Who is it? Whose car?

WOMAN. The schoolteacher. Mr Ryder. His body wrapped around the tree. His clothes blown clean from his back.

POLICEMAN. Does anyone know where Mrs Ryder is? She ought to be told. Anyone know where Mrs Ryder is?

HORTENSE (*suddenly*). I know where Mrs Ryder is!

The crowd turns to look at her.

Mrs Ryder is in the schoolhouse, kissing Michael Roberts!

Gasps and consternation erupt amongst the crowd.

Morning. The house. MISS JEWEL *is sitting at the table, rocking backwards and forwards. In another room,* MISS MA *is crying.* HORTENSE *enters.*

MISS JEWEL (*relieved*). Oh, it you, me sprigadee. Oh, where you bin nah?

HORTENSE. I took shelter for the night. What's happening?

MISS JEWEL. The boy he done a bad ting. A bad ting.

MISS MA enters. Her hair is dishevelled, her face streaked with tears.

MISS MA (*to* HORTENSE). Where have you been?

HORTENSE. I…

MISS MA. Were you at the schoolhouse? Were you?!

HORTENSE. I was there yesterday. I…

MISS MA. They are saying that my son was caught in an unholy embrace with that woman! Did you know what he was doing with her? (*Grabbing* HORTENSE *and shaking her.*) Did you know?

HORTENSE. No! Why are you shouting at me? Why is this my fault?!

There is a commotion outside. MICHAEL *enters the house. He shouts back at the small crowd of* REPORTERS *and* LOCALS *who have been following him –*

MICHAEL. Go away! There's nothing to see! Yeah, yeah! Nothing to see!

He looks at them, taking in their shattered expressions.

You'd think there would be bigger stories today. Even in this sad little town.

They are silent.

Where's Papa?

MISS MA. Lying down. He's…

MICHAEL. You'd better fetch him. Tell him I'm leaving.

MISS MA. What…?

MICHAEL. I'm going to England. There's going to be a war, you know? I will join the Royal Air Force. Fight for the Mother Country.

MISS MA. No. No. You can't. What are you talking about? You can't go…

MR PHILIP *enters. He can barely hold himself upright.*

MR PHILIP. Let him go. He is not welcome in this house. He has brought shame on my name. Shame on this family. Let him go.

Pause. MICHAEL *stares at his father. For a moment it seems he might ask his forgiveness, but –*

MICHAEL. Fine by me, Papa.

MICHAEL *walks past* MR PHILIP *and out of the room.*

MISS MA. No! No!

In MICHAEL*'s room.* MICHAEL *is throwing some things in a case.* HORTENSE *enters. He doesn't look at her.*

HORTENSE. Is she going with you? To England?

MICHAEL. Who?

HORTENSE. Mrs Ryder. Stella.

MICHAEL. Course not. She's with her God folk. She'll be back in New Jersey by the end of the week.

HORTENSE. I don't understand...

MICHAEL. I wouldn't expect you to. Do yourself a favour, Hortense – get away from this house, from this small, small town as fast as your legs can take you. There is a whole world out there where real things are happening and people are really living their lives.

HORTENSE. If by that you mean forgetting all God's teaching, and losing all your morality, and standards, then thank you, but I would prefer to stay at home.

Pause.

MICHAEL. You sound like Papa.

Goodbye, Hortense.

He stands looking at her, his suitcase in his hand. She won't look at him.

(*Hopefully.*) I'm sorry.

He waits but she says nothing. He leaves. HORTENSE *can't move. She listens to him leaving as her heart breaks. In the next room,* MISS MA *can be heard sobbing –*

MISS MA. Michael. Michael!

Scene Two

Winter. 1941.

Pathé-style news footage of 'The Blitz Spirit' – proud Londoners staying cheerful and helping each other out in the face of Hitler's devastating bombing raids.

On the stage, the old-fashioned, dowdy living room of a large house in Earl's Court. Two VOLUNTEERS *in overalls are standing at either end of a bedstead, trying to carry it towards the door. They are being blocked by* BERNARD. QUEENIE *is in the middle of the room.*

BERNARD. No!

QUEENIE. Bernard...

BERNARD. I have said no. (*To* VOLUNTEER.) Let go of it!

QUEENIE. But, Bernard, we'll get it back. We're just lending it. It's doing nothing upstairs, just sitting in those rooms covered in newspaper. It's a couple of beds, a table and four...

The VOLUNTEERS *try to move towards the door again.*

BERNARD. No! Stop! Let... go!

QUEENIE. Oh, for goodness' sake! It's just for a few months. They'll give it back...

BERNARD. Who will? Who?

QUEENIE. Dora and her family – Mrs Palmer. They came into the rest centre. They've been bombed out and...

BERNARD. Oh for... No!

QUEENIE. Her husband's in the hospital. They've been given a flat but they haven't got a stick of...

BERNARD. Are they our sort of people?

QUEENIE. What do you...?

BERNARD. Are they? Or are they like that last bunch you dragged in here trying to help with their... lice-ridden children and...

QUEENIE. Oh, we'd all be lice-ridden if we'd been bombed out in the East End...

BERNARD. We most certainly would not!

QUEENIE (*to audience*). To be honest, I'm actually enjoying this. This is the most lively Bernard's been since I married him – since I met him. If only I'd known it takes furniture to get him going. (*Watching him.*) Look at him. He's so furious that the vein in his temple that annoys me when he eats is pumping away like it's got a heart of its own.

QUEENIE *suddenly grabs a chair, provocatively, and hands it to a* VOLUNTEER –

(*To* VOLUNTEER.) Take it to the van.

BERNARD. No! (*To* VOLUNTEERS.) Put that down! You will not take it. I have said no!

QUEENIE (*to audience*). How did I end up here? In this lanky house in Earl's Court, married to a fella I've as much in common with as a creature from another planet? It's not what I imagined for myself. But then again, I don't come from a place where you do much imagining. Growing up, I knew just one thing – that I didn't want to spend my whole life on that stinking farm, with my dad butchering the animals in the shed, helping my mother with the meat pies, swilling out the blood from my brothers' overalls. Maid of all drudgery, that was me.

I'll tell you the story of my deliverance. It came in an unlikely form.

Enter AUNTIE DOROTHY, *a large, titivated woman, and* MR AND MRS BUXTON – QUEENIE's *parents.* QUEENIE *goes to join them in the farmhouse kitchen.*

DOROTHY. The shop's getting too much for me now that my poor dear Montgomery's gone. It's very difficult when you've been treated like a princess for twenty-five years, to find yourself alone again and with everything to do. It's a nice little earner, mind. And I do newspapers now as well as the sweets and tobacco. But I can't cope with being on my feet all day. Not with my bunions as they are...

MRS BUXTON. You should try wearing proper shoes, Dot. I've always said so.

DOROTHY. So I've been thinking about taking on a shop assistant. I did start looking for someone locally, but then I thought – what about my niece, Queenie?

There is a shocked silence.

I wonder if she might like to come and live in London for a while and help her poor auntie out?

MR BUXTON. You what?

QUEENIE. Me?

DOROTHY. I'd pay you a small wage as well as your board and lodging. We'd have to sort you out with some pretty clothes to wear. Do you always dress like that?

MR BUXTON. She's been cleaning out the chicken sheds. What else is she supposed to wear?

QUEENIE. I have got one nice dress – my Sunday dress.

DOROTHY. Well, we could go on a little shopping expedition to Oxford Street. Ooh, I would enjoy that.

QUEENIE (*transported*). So would I.

MR BUXTON. Now just a minute. We need her here.

MRS BUXTON. It's the pies you see. She's up helping me at dawn and we've to work fast if we're to...

QUEENIE. But couldn't you get someone from the village? A miner's daughter like you did when I was little...

MRS BUXTON. Oh, you know what they're like. They never put the jelly in right. I've always to be watching them and...

QUEENIE. Mum, please. You know I don't like working on the farm. I wish I did but...

MR BUXTON. I should have seen this coming. Ever since you announced that you're a vegetarian.

QUEENIE. I am a vegetarian.

MR BUXTON. Have you ever heard the like? Queenie Bee –
our meat's not good enough for the likes of her.

MRS BUXTON. Now then. She didn't say that.

MR BUXTON (*to* QUEENIE). You're a butcher's daughter,
from a long line of butchers. It's supposed to be in your blood!

QUEENIE. Well, it's not in my blood!

Pause.

DOROTHY. Oh, dear. I can see I've put the cat amongst the
pigeons.

QUEENIE. You haven't. You haven't, Auntie.

Mum. Dad. Please.

*Two weeks later. A fitting room in a department store,
Oxford Street.* QUEENIE *is behind a screen with a shop
assistant, putting on new clothes.* DOROTHY *is sitting on
a chair on the other side of the screen, eating coconut ice
from a paper bag.*

DOROTHY. Are you going to show me?

QUEENIE. Almost there.

QUEENIE *steps out from behind the screen. She's wearing a
yellow cardigan over a floral dress.*

DOROTHY. Oh! Oh, you do scrub up well. I knew you would.
Yellow's definitely your colour.

QUEENIE. Is it?

DOROTHY. Oh, yes. Turn round.

QUEENIE *does so.*

Yes. (*To the* ASSISTANT.) We'll take both. And we'll take a
cardigan in pink as well.

QUEENIE. Are you sure, Auntie?

DOROTHY. Quite sure. You look a proper confection. Leave
them on. We'll go and have cake to celebrate.

I can see I'm going to have to be careful with you. I shall lose you as soon as I've found you. You'll be snapped up by some lucky young admirer.

QUEENIE (*embarrassed*). Auntie.

DOROTHY. You will, you know. You'd like that, wouldn't you? A nice young gentleman to walk out with?

Later. QUEENIE*'s room above the shop.* QUEENIE *stands in front of a dressing table with three mirrors.*

QUEENIE (*to audience*). It turned out I would. Once I'd made my escape I found myself thinking about all sorts of possibilities in that department. I knew what went on of course – you can't grow up on a farm and not know. I'd even been asked out once or twice by some snotty-nosed miners' lads who I'd laughed at. But I'd been to the pictures too. I'd seen those movie stars with beautiful powdered faces and glossy curls. I knew there was such a thing as romance. What if that could happen to me? What if I could be adored, pursued? I could get married, have a home of my own, have babies. Babies. When my brothers were very little it'd been my job to look after them. I can still remember how they felt in my arms, the warmth of them, the softness of their little necks and hands.

QUEENIE *looks at her reflection in the mirrors, repositioning them for a better view.*

I had a proper bedroom at Auntie's house – in the rooms above the shop. I had a dressing table. I could see hundreds of Queenies – pretty, grown-up. (*Amazed.*) This was me.

A week later. The shop. QUEENIE *goes to stand behind the counter.*

The first time Bernard came into the shop, I hardly noticed him.

QUEENIE *is serving a* YOUNG MAN *when* BERNARD *enters. He is wearing his gaberdine coat and hat.*

YOUNG MAN. Go on – I'll take two ounces of Cherry Lips as well.

QUEENIE *reaches for the jar of Cherry Lips from the shelf. The* YOUNG MAN *makes a show of watching her skirt ride up slightly at the back. He winks at* BERNARD, *who looks away quickly.* QUEENIE *weighs out the sweets and puts them in a bag.*

(*To* QUEENIE.) I bet your lips taste like cherries.

QUEENIE. You're not likely to find out.

YOUNG MAN. You're new here, aren't you? What's your name? Let me guess – 'Sugarbaby'? 'Sweetheart'? Get it?

QUEENIE. It's Queenie.

YOUNG MAN. Queenie! Well, if you ever need a handsome prince to sweep you off your feet, I'm your man. See ya.

The YOUNG MAN *leaves.* BERNARD *steps forward, shyly.*

QUEENIE. How can I help you?

BERNARD. I was... I'm looking for *The...*

QUEENIE. *The Times?*

BERNARD (*blushing*). Yes. Yes, thank you. I will take *The Times.*

She hands it to him and he gives her the money.

QUEENIE. Thank you.

BERNARD. Good day.

QUEENIE. Good day.

BERNARD *leaves.* DOROTHY *appears from the room behind the shop.*

DOROTHY. Did I just hear someone ask for *The Times?*

QUEENIE. Yes.

DOROTHY. Ooh! That'll be a proper gentleman then. No spivs or cockneys ever read *The Times.* What did he look like?

QUEENIE. Er... Tall. Skinny. Not bad looking.

DOROTHY. Ooh! We shall have to watch out for him! Fetch me some more coconut ice, will you?

QUEENIE (*to audience*). The second time he came in...

The following morning. QUEENIE *is behind the counter when* BERNARD *enters.*

BERNARD (*tipping his hat*). Good morning.

QUEENIE. Good morning. *The Times*?

BERNARD. Yes. Thank you.

QUEENIE *gives him the paper.*

Rather inclement for the time of year.

QUEENIE. What's that?

BERNARD (*blushing*). The weather – rather cloudy.

QUEENIE. Oh. Yes. It is.

He gives her the money.

Thank you.

BERNARD. Good day.

QUEENIE. Good day.

BERNARD *leaves.*

(*To audience.*) The third time he came in, he just came straight out with it – like he'd been practising.

BERNARD *enters.*

BERNARD. I wonder if you would care to come for a walk with me tomorrow afternoon. In the park. I've been assured it's to be a lovely day.

QUEENIE *is shocked and speechless for a moment.*

DOROTHY (*from back room*). Yes!

BERNARD. Good. I'll call for you at one.

He turns to leave then stops, emboldened.

I'm sorry, but I don't believe we've ever been introduced. Bernard Bligh.

QUEENIE. My name's...

BERNARD. Queenie. Yes. I know. Good day.

QUEENIE. Good day.

The following afternoon. QUEENIE *and* BERNARD *sit down on a park bench. They are silent for a moment.* QUEENIE *takes a paper bag from her pocket and holds it out to him –*

Liquorice?

BERNARD. Oh. (*Taking a piece.*) Thank you.

QUEENIE *watches him eat from the corner of her eye.*

QUEENIE (*to audience*). There's that vein in his temple. Why does it have to move around like that? Like a worm under his skin.

(*To* BERNARD.) Do you live close by?

BERNARD. About fifteen minutes' walk – (*Pointing.*) in that direction. Nevern Street.

Pause.

QUEENIE. Where do you work?

BERNARD. Lloyd's Bank. Clerk.

QUEENIE. Do you like it?

BERNARD. It's a solid job. Some prospects, I like to think.

Pause.

QUEENIE. Do you live on your own?

BERNARD. With my father. He was in the Great War. He's… He has what they call 'shell shock'.

QUEENIE. Oh, dear. Shame. My dad tried to sign up but they wouldn't have him. Weak heart.

BERNARD *nods slightly. Pause.*

(*To audience.*) They say 'Silence is Golden', but this one was in danger of being burnt to a crisp.

(*To* BERNARD.) I grew up on a farm. In Lincolnshire…

BERNARD. Oh.

QUEENIE (*to audience*). I ended up telling him anything and everything I could think of, nattering away until it was time to go home.

They stand, and walk back to the shop.

BERNARD (*tipping his hat*). Thank you. May I call for you on Sunday? Around two?

QUEENIE. Yes. If you like.

Some weeks later, QUEENIE *is in the shop with* DOROTHY.

But he never says anything. Except about the weather. It's been over two months now and I hardly know anything about him.

DOROTHY. He's reserved. That's a sure sign of him being a gentleman. Does he open doors for you?

QUEENIE. Yes.

DOROTHY. Does he walk on the outside of you when you're going down the road?

QUEENIE. Yes.

DOROTHY. That's so you don't get splashed by a carriage.

QUEENIE. When did you last get splashed by a carriage? He's odd. You should see him when he's counting out his money to pay for tea – checking each coin, putting them down in little piles. It's like he's backward.

DOROTHY. Oh, don't be daft. You've found yourself a little gem, Queenie. You'll be safe as houses with him.

QUEENIE. You don't think we're courting, do you?

DOROTHY. Of course you're courting!

QUEENIE. But... I thought... Don't people get all dreamy when they're courting?

DOROTHY. Oh, you don't want to bother with any of that.

QUEENIE. I don't know. I don't know. It doesn't feel right.

The following day. QUEENIE *and* BERNARD *are sitting in the cinema together. All around them, young couples are kissing and fondling each other. On the screen, a glamorous couple is kissing passionately in the last scene of the film. Sweeping music as the film finishes. The lights come up and* QUEENIE *and* BERNARD *sit awkwardly as the couples around them gradually extricate themselves from each other and straighten their clothes before starting to leave.*

Bernard... I've enjoyed our little outings but I don't think we should see each other any more.

He looks at her, shocked. Then his face collapses and his lip starts to quiver.

BERNARD. No, Queenie, please don't say that. This... this means a lot to me.

QUEENIE. Oh. I didn't think you'd be upset...

BERNARD. I really am very fond of you. I know I'm older than you and perhaps not as lively as you'd like. But over these months...

He turns away, overcome.

QUEENIE. It's just...

BERNARD (*suddenly taking hold of her hand*). Please, please don't say any more. Just give me another chance. I was hoping to persuade you that... that we should get engaged.

Pause.

QUEENIE. Oh. Well... It's something to think about perhaps. Well. Never mind then. I'll see you again on Thursday.

She stands. He stands immediately.

BERNARD. Yes. Thursday. Thank you.

He suddenly kisses her on the cheek – a pecky sort of kiss.

QUEENIE (*to audience*). In the end it was a tragedy that brought things to a head.

In the shop, DOROTHY *falls down dead.*

A week later, it's DOROTHY*'s funeral.* MR BUXTON *and other family members carry the coffin containing* DOROTHY *to the graveyard.* BERNARD *joins them, putting his shoulder under the coffin to help bear the heavy weight.*

QUEENIE *and* MRS BUXTON *look on as the men put the coffin down.*

MRS BUXTON. Eh, dear. Death by coconut ice.

QUEENIE. Yes.

MRS BUXTON. I suppose that's it now then. The shop'll be sold. Never mind – you can come back home now. There's plenty for you to do around the farm.

QUEENIE. What? Not on your nelly, Mother.

MRS BUXTON. But…

QUEENIE. No.

She looks at where BERNARD *is now shaking hands with* MR BUXTON – *like a regular man.*

Actually, I've some good news for you. I'm getting married, Mother. To Bernard Bligh.

Six weeks later. QUEENIE *and* BERNARD *enter the front room of his house in Nevern Street.* BERNARD *is carrying* QUEENIE*'s large suitcase.* ARTHUR, BERNARD*'s father, is sitting by the fireplace. He stands and walks towards* QUEENIE.

BERNARD. Queenie, this is my father – Arthur.

ARTHUR *holds his hand out shyly and they shake hands.*

QUEENIE. Hello. It's very nice to meet you at last.

ARTHUR *brings her a chair. She smiles and sits down.*

Thank you.

Pause. QUEENIE *takes in the room, which is dingy and unloved.*

It's a big place you've got here.

BERNARD. Three stories. But we only use four rooms. Since Mother died.

QUEENIE. When was that?

BERNARD. Fifteen years ago.

QUEENIE. Well, perhaps we can open things up a bit...

BERNARD. I'm not sure about...

QUEENIE. I could give the whole place a clean from top to bottom. Get some more light in. I think we could make it proper grand.

BERNARD. Father, would you put the kettle on?

ARTHUR *exits to the kitchen.*

Queenie, before we go upstairs... I've rather made an assumption that we'll be sleeping in the same bed. I hope...

QUEENIE. Oh, yes. Yes. That's fine.

BERNARD. Queenie, I probably should have said this before we got married, but... I would like children.

QUEENIE. Yes. Good. So would I.

He smiles. He pats her on the shoulder.

(*To audience*.) He's very polite about it – 'relations'. He unties his pyjama bottoms and bunches the fabric into his hand so they don't drop down and spoil the surprise.

BERNARD. Darling?

QUEENIE. He always asks like that. Then he gets in bed and pulls up my nightie under the covers until he can slip his hand between my legs and part them. Then he rolls on top of me, fumbles about like he's searching for a light switch in the dark, and sticks it in. A held breath that turns him pink, a grunt, spittle all down my neck, and then it's over.

There's been no babies yet. I even went to the doctor's a couple of months back to see if he could help. 'I take it you are having normal conjugal relations, Mrs Bligh? Do you relax? Do you enjoy it?' 'Not so's you'd notice.' I said. He told me to go back home and try harder.

*The front room, Nevern Street. We are back where we began.
The* VOLUNTEERS *still have hold of the bedstead.*

BERNARD. Queenie! Are you listening to me?

QUEENIE. Yes.

BERNARD. It isn't even our furniture to give away. My mother
and father bought that furniture. Some of it's even handed
down from...

QUEENIE. Right. Right. Let's ask Arthur, shall we – see what
he thinks. (*Calling.*) Arthur! Arthur, can you come here?

BERNARD. Oh, don't be... you know he can't say...

QUEENIE. Course he can. He's not daft.

ARTHUR *enters from the kitchen.* QUEENIE *and*
BERNARD *speak over one another –*

Arthur, there's a family at the Rest Centre...

BERNARD. She has no idea what they'll do with it...

QUEENIE....who have absolutely nothing. Lost it all in a bomb.
Can we lend them a bed or two...

BERNARD....And she knows nothing about these people.

QUEENIE. A chair to sit down on. They've got kids, Arthur.
Can we?

ARTHUR *nods decisively.*

Good. Right. (*To* VOLUNTEERS.) Take it to the van please.

The VOLUNTEERS *carry the bedstead out.* BERNARD *is
quiet for a moment, profoundly disturbed.*

BERNARD. I want something in writing. A contract.

QUEENIE. Oh, for goodness' sake.

BERNARD. You're too trusting. You can't help everyone. Isn't
it enough that you're working at that Rest Centre day and
night? You're worn out...

QUEENIE. There's a war on, Bernard.

BERNARD. I am aware of that.

QUEENIE. Are you? Because there's thousands of people out there having much more of a war than you are.

Silence. BERNARD *looks like he's been slapped. He turns away.* QUEENIE *regrets what she's said –*

Look… Bernard…

The air-raid siren suddenly begins to wail loudly.

Oh, no! No! (*Shouting upwards.*) Could you not just give it a rest for one night?!

ARTHUR *has begun to shake all over.*

BERNARD (*looking around*). Where's his gas mask?

QUEENIE. It's all right, Arthur.

The planes are heard overhead.

BERNARD. We have to go to the shelter, Father.

QUEENIE. They're coming already. What sort of a warning's that?

ARTHUR *has dived under the table.* BERNARD *goes to pull him out.*

BERNARD. Father!

QUEENIE. It's too late. Forget the shelter.

BERNARD. No. He has to…

QUEENIE. Just get down, will you?

QUEENIE *and* BERNARD *scramble under the table next to* ARTHUR, *as the noise of the planes grows louder.*

BERNARD. We should go to the shelter.

QUEENIE. They're close by.

BERNARD. Oh, God. Oh, God.

Terrified, BERNARD *begins to tremble. Suddenly there is a tremendous whistling sound.*

QUEENIE. Oh, no!

There is a huge, deafening explosion. ARTHUR *curls up into a tiny ball.* BERNARD *just manages to cling onto the leg of the table.* QUEENIE *is thrown backwards by the blast, banging her head on the floor. Pieces of debris begin to rain down onto the roof of the house. Slowly,* QUEENIE *manages to sit up, dizzy and shocked.*

BERNARD (*shaking*). That was the roof. Oh, God...

QUEENIE. I don't think it was us.

BERNARD. The whole thing's going to come down. It's going to come down...

QUEENIE. It's all right, Bernard. It's all right. I'll go and look...

She starts to move but BERNARD *suddenly grabs her and pulls her back to him, holding her tightly.*

BERNARD. No! No. No. No. Not you. Not you. Never. Never. Never you.

The sound of the falling debris gradually stops. BERNARD *gradually loosens his grasp on* QUEENIE.

QUEENIE. It was close but I'm sure it wasn't us. It wasn't us. It's all right. (*Stroking his head.*) There, there. There, there.

BERNARD *manages to breathe. He fights back tears.* QUEENIE *crawls out from under the table. She stands, shakily, and makes her way to the window. She lifts a corner of the blackout curtain and peers out.*

BERNARD. I want you to know, Queenie – I do love you.

QUEENIE *looks back at him, astonished. This is the first time he's said that. She watches him as he goes to* ARTHUR *and helps him up from the floor.*

Three days later. The Rest Centre. There are desperate people everywhere, waiting to be seen. One of QUEENIE*'s colleagues,* FRANNY, *approaches her –*

FRANNY. Here – have some PC3s.

QUEENIE. I'm that tired I don't know if I'm coming or going. (*Of the people waiting*.) Look at them all.

FRANNY. Best not. Just look at the next one in front of you. Oh, I've got a favour to ask – didn't you say you've some spare rooms in your house?

QUEENIE. Yes, but...

FRANNY. Could you put a flight crew up for a couple of nights? End of next week? It's just three of them. My sister's sweet on one of them and if they stay locally...

QUEENIE. Franny, I can't. Bernard won't have it...

FRANNY. They're none of your rubbish. Proper flyers. 103 Squadron Lancasters. They've only got three days' leave...

QUEENIE. I'm sorry. You know I would if I could.

FRANNY. Ah, well. Worth a try.

BERNARD enters. QUEENIE sees him at once and looks surprised. She leaves FRANNY and goes to BERNARD.

QUEENIE. What are you doing here? Is something wrong? It's not Arthur, is it?

BERNARD. No. But I need to speak to you. And you didn't come home last night, or the night before so...

QUEENIE. Sorry. It just wasn't worth trying to get back. We've been that busy. And with the streets as they are...

BERNARD. I've signed up.

Pause. QUEENIE is shocked.

RAF. Boys in blue.

QUEENIE. Oh. Is this because of what I said the other day? I didn't...

BERNARD. You were right. Can't leave it any longer. Have to do my bit.

QUEENIE. But... are you not too old?

BERNARD. Apparently not. Keen to have me. Won't be flying of course – eyesight. But I go up to Skegness for basic training. Then I'll be shipped out.

QUEENIE. When?

BERNARD. Tomorrow morning.

So, you'll come home tonight?

QUEENIE. Yes.

BERNARD. Good.

BERNARD leaves.

The following morning. The sitting room, Nevern Street. QUEENIE watches as BERNARD fastens his coat.

QUEENIE. I wonder where you'll be sent.

You will write?

BERNARD. Of course.

About Father... I know it's a lot to ask...

QUEENIE. It's fine. We'll be fine. You'll be back before we know it.

She suddenly takes his hand. For a moment, she feels she will cry. They look down at their clasped hands, unable to say anything. ARTHUR enters. BERNARD picks up his bag.

BERNARD. Right.

He goes to ARTHUR and shakes his hand.

Goodbye, Father.

ARTHUR nods sadly. BERNARD goes to QUEENIE and pecks her on the cheek.

Goodbye.

QUEENIE. Bye, then.

BERNARD leaves. QUEENIE notices that ARTHUR is crying –

Look on the bright side, Arthur – he's that thin the enemy'll have a job to hit him. Especially if he turns sideways.

ARTHUR *suddenly laughs, silently.*

That's tickled you, has it? Come on. Let's get the kettle on.

A week later. ARTHUR *is sitting in the living room. The front-door bell rings. He crouches down behind the chair.*

QUEENIE *calls to him from the kitchen –*

(*Off.*) Arthur, that'll be them! Answer the door, will you!

After a moment, she enters. She's wearing an apron and drying her hands.

Oh, Arthur. It's just the front door.

She exits towards the hall. ARTHUR *comes out from his hiding place.*

QUEENIE *returns with two airmen –* KIP *and* GINGER.

KIP. I hope you were expecting us, Mrs Bligh.

QUEENIE. Call me Queenie. I was told there'd be three of you.

GINGER. Yes – there's one more just coming.

QUEENIE. Good. Because I've made up three beds. This is my father-in-law, Arthur.

KIP *and* GINGER. How do you do, sir?

QUEENIE. He doesn't speak.

The front-door bell rings.

GINGER. Shall I get it?

QUEENIE. Why not? Make yourself at home.

GINGER *exits to the hall.*

KIP. That's Ginger, by the way. And I'm Kip.

QUEENIE. Sleep a lot, do you?

KIP. Short for Kipling. My mother loves him. She also loves Trollope so I got off lightly.

GINGER *enters –*

GINGER. Here we are.

MICHAEL *enters behind* GINGER. QUEENIE *and*
ARTHUR *stare at him in astonishment – they have never*
seen a black man before. But then MICHAEL *speaks –*

MICHAEL. Good evening. This is really very kind of you,
Mrs Bligh. I'm Michael. Flight Sergeant Michael Roberts.

– and QUEENIE *feels something else – a profound and*
instant attraction. She smiles at MICHAEL *shyly, and*
MICHAEL *smiles back.*

Scene Three

Autumn 1943.

Pathé-style images of Jamaicans and other West Indians joining
the British war effort – excited, willing and proud.

On the stage, the auditorium of a cinema in a town in
Lincolnshire. The film has been stopped and, on the white screen,
the end of the reel is flickering. A vicious, chaotic fist-fight has
broken out between a group of BLACK G.I.*s and a group of*
WHITE G.I.*s. Caught in amongst it are a number of* CIVILIANS
– some cowering, some joining in. The CINEMA MANAGER *is*
running about, trying but failing to regain control.

Centre stage, GILBERT JOSEPH, *a Jamaican RAF recruit, is*
brawling with a WHITE G.I. *The action freezes.* GILBERT
looks at the audience and sucks his teeth.

GILBERT (*to audience*). My mother always say that violence
solve nothing. And I always say she's right. But, man, I got
to confess to you – right now, this feels good.

The fight resumes. GILBERT *is getting the better of his*
opponent. Near to GILBERT, *an* OLD LADY *starts hitting*
a WHITE G.I. *with her handbag. The action freezes again.*

(*To audience.*) One part of my brain is saying, 'Gilbert, you
will be made to pay dearly for this moment of profound

satisfaction.' But, man, this the sweetest moment of my war so far.

Please don't judge me yet. Allow me to explain. Let me take you back to the RAF recruiting office in Kingston on the day I sign up.

Enter, two RAF RECRUITING OFFICERS. GILBERT *stands before them, nervous but excited.*

OFFICER 1 (*referring to a form in his hand*). So. Gilbert Joseph.

GILBERT. That's me.

OFFICER 1. Born in Jamaica. Both your parents British-Jamaican?

GILBERT. Yes, sir. Although my father is Jewish. Was Jewish. I don't know if that...

OFFICER 2. Good Lord! I didn't know there were any Jews in Jamaica.

GILBERT. Oh, yes, sir. There are quite a number of Jews here. But my father is a Christian now. Ever since he met Jesus on the battlefield at Ypres. He says the Lord shared a tin of fish with him and lent him some writing paper. He only says this when he's drunk, mind.

OFFICER 1. Well. Jewish heritage. Even more reason to join the fight against Herr Hitler.

GILBERT. Yes, sir.

OFFICER 1. You've passed some exams, I see.

GILBERT. Yes. At St John's College. It is my plan to go to a university and study the Law. I mean to be a lawyer.

OFFICER 2. Do you?

OFFICER 1. Excellent. Well, you're certainly the sort of chap we need. With these grades we'll be getting you trained up as a wireless operator, an air gunner. Perhaps a flight engineer – second only to a pilot in terms of respect. How does that sound?

GILBERT (*delighted and surprised*). That sound fine, sir.

OFFICER 1. Then after the war, with an impressive service record, I think Civvy Street will positively welcome you for further study.

He stands. GILBERT *stands too.* OFFICER 1 *shakes* GILBERT*'s hand.*

Congratulations. Good man.

A week later, in his parents' house, GILBERT *is trying on his RAF jacket. His cousin,* ELWOOD, *is beside him, shaking his head in disbelief.*

ELWOOD. Why you wanna go licky-licky to the British?

GILBERT (*to audience*). This is my cousin – Elwood.

ELWOOD. Cha, this a white man's war. Why you wanna lose your life for a white man?

GILBERT. Have you heard what this Hitler fellow is saying? He is saying we are like monkeys. 'Anthropoid.' I looked it up in the dictionary – 'Resembling a human but primitive like an ape.'

ELWOOD. Lose your life for Jamaica. Independence – that is worth a fight. Lose your life to see a black man in the Governor's house doing more than just sweeping the floor. This war will change nothing for you and me.

GILBERT. It will get me off this island for one thing. And I will be an air gunner. And I will go to an English university.

ELWOOD. Is that what they tell you? Man, the English are liars. They tell you anything to make you do their dirty work.

GILBERT *ignores him and puts on his cap.*

GILBERT. Elwood, I tell you what this is about – you are jealous.

ELWOOD. What?!

GILBERT. Look at me and tell me honestly that I do not look devastatingly handsome in this blue uniform.

ELWOOD (*laughing*). What?!

GILBERT. Tell me the women are not going to take one look at me and fall down at my feet.

ELWOOD. You kidding me!

GILBERT. Now come. The bar is waiting. You can use me as bait.

(*To audience*.) Now I will show you what happened when I finally arrived in England after my basic training. I was posted to an RAF camp in a place called Lincolnshire.

Enter a group of WEST INDIAN RECRUITS *who are shivering and miserable.* GILBERT *goes to stand with them. Enter* FLIGHT SERGEANT THWAITES. *The* RECRUITS *salute, reluctantly.*

SERGEANT. At ease. Stop shivering!

GILBERT (*to audience*). This is Flight Sergeant Thwaites, better known to us recruits as Sergeant Bastard.

SERGEANT. Right, airmen. You lot are being remustered for trade training. As of today.

GILBERT. What...?

SERGEANT. We need ground staff, and plenty of them. Pronto.

Some of the RECRUITS *suck their teeth.*

Stop that!

GILBERT. I think there has been some mistake, Sergeant. When I joined up I was told I would be an air gunner, or a wireless operator or...

SERGEANT. This is a war not a shop.

GILBERT. I was told a posting overseas.

SERGEANT. Well you are overseas, aren't you? Bingo. A little bird tells me you can drive a car, Joseph. That right?

GILBERT. Drive?

SERGEANT. Yes. You know – brum, brum, beep, beep.

GILBERT. No, sir. How would I have learned to drive? No cars where I come from, sir.

SERGEANT. Driving since the age of ten – that's what I heard.

GILBERT. No, Flight Sergeant. That is someone else.

SERGEANT. Stop taking the piss, Joseph.

GILBERT. I...

SERGEANT. Motor Transport. Dismissed.

GILBERT (*to audience*). Man, I could almost hear Elwood laughing. Six months of driving a coal truck. Six months of driving to railway stations and shovelling that filthy stuff around. It felt like a punishment. Coal dust in my hair, under my clothes, lungs thick with silt. I tell you, I lived for my few hours off.

Sometimes, my comrades and I would walk into the village near the camp. The first time we saunter down that pretty little main street –

GILBERT *and some of the other* WEST INDIAN RECRUITS *begin to walk down the main street of a village. The* LOCALS *stop and stare. Silence descends.*

(*To audience.*) It wasn't hostility – more a mix of amazement and curiosity and fear. I swear, if they'd had a stick long enough they would have poked us with it.

A WOMAN *holding a baby dares to approach.*

WOMAN. Hello.

GILBERT. Good afternoon.

WOMAN (*calling to the other* LOCALS). They do speak English!

(*To* GILBERT.) Where you from, then?

GILBERT. The West Indies, ma'am.

WOMAN. The what now? Is that in Africa?

The baby begins to cry. The WOMAN *retreats.*

GILBERT (*to audience*). Africa? How come they know nothing about their own empire? Two weeks ago, I came into the village on my own.

GILBERT *goes to sit down on a bench in a quiet spot, opens his newspaper and starts to read.*

ARTHUR *approaches cautiously and stands a few feet away from* GILBERT, *staring at him. He is wearing a shabby coat and his hands fidget constantly.* GILBERT *looks up and notices him, but then goes back to reading his paper.* ARTHUR *moves a step closer.* GILBERT *looks up again.* ARTHUR *stares at him, wide-eyed.*

Is there something I can do for you, sir?

ARTHUR *doesn't reply.* GILBERT *tries to read again but he's aware of* ARTHUR*'s gaze.*

Can I help you?

No reply.

You want this bench – is that it?

ARTHUR *doesn't reply, but his eyes are full of a sort of earnest entreaty.*

(*Standing.*) There. It is all yours. You are most welcome.

GILBERT *sucks his teeth and folds his newspaper. He starts to walk away, but* ARTHUR *follows him.* GILBERT *stops and looks back. He takes in the fact that* ARTHUR *is behind him, then turns and starts to walk again. A plane can be heard approaching in the sky, as* GILBERT *decides to confront* ARTHUR.

(*Not unkindly.*) What is it you want, sir? You want to touch my black skin for luck – is that it?

At this moment, the plane flies low overhead – a damaged Lancaster trying to make it back to the air base, its engine struggling. GILBERT *looks up and waves his arms –*

Go, boy! You can make it! Go, boy!

As the plane disappears, GILBERT *looks back towards* ARTHUR *and sees that he has thrown himself flat on the ground. He is covering his ears and shaking violently.*

Oh, man! (*Approaching* ARTHUR *cautiously.*) You all right, man?

ARTHUR *scrambles to his feet, muddied and shaking.*
GILBERT *looks around but there's no one to help.*

Calm yourself, now, man. Don't want people thinking I've
harmed you. You all right?

No reply.

What is it you want? Tell me.

ARTHUR *plunges his hand deep into his trouser pocket and
starts rummaging around.*

What!? Nuh! You dirty, dirty little…

ARTHUR *produces a piece of crumpled paper and holds it
out to* GILBERT.

(*Relieved.*) Oh.

GILBERT *approaches* ARTHUR *and takes the paper.*
ARTHUR *jumps back a few feet.* GILBERT *unfolds the
paper and reads it –*

'My name is Arthur Bligh. If you find me please return me to
21, Nevern Street, Earl's Court, London SW5.' London? You
a very long way from home.

ARTHUR*'s eyes widen and he stares at the paper.* GILBERT
turns it over.

Ah. 'Please return me to Hollishead Farm, Honington…'
I know that place – I've passed it a few times.

GILBERT *checks his watch. He sucks his teeth and makes
a decision.*

Come on then, Arthur. We better do what it say.

The Buxtons' farm. GILBERT *approaches the farmhouse
door with* ARTHUR *on his heels. He's about to knock, when*
QUEENIE *suddenly rushes from the house, excitedly –*

QUEENIE. Sergeant Michael Rob– …

She stops in her tracks on seeing GILBERT*'s face.*

(*Disappointed.*) Oh.

GILBERT. It's all right, madam. I don't mean you any harm.
I...

QUEENIE (*looking at* ARTHUR). Where did you find him?

GILBERT. In the village. He wouldn't leave me alone. Started
following me.

ARTHUR *is grinning at* QUEENIE, *proudly.*

QUEENIE. Did he now? (*To* ARTHUR.) It's not him, you daft
beggar. Inside now, Arthur. And get those mucky boots off.

ARTHUR – *crestfallen* – *goes past her into the house.*

GILBERT (*to audience*). Now I, like every Jamaican man, am
adept at taking in the whole spectacle of a woman in the
blink of an unsuspecting eye. It is hard to say whether this is
a training or a natural-born gift. This woman was so lovely
I wanted to rub my hands together and kiss the crazy man
who brought me to this place.

QUEENIE. Sorry. He brought you home for me. He thinks
you're someone else.

GILBERT. Don't tell me – Paul Robeson.

QUEENIE. Paul Robeson? You think a lot of yourself, don't you?
Anyway, he wouldn't know Paul Robeson if he fell on him.

GILBERT. Madam, if Paul Robeson were to fall upon him,
there would have been no need for you to come to the door –
I could have posted the gentleman underneath.

QUEENIE (*suppressing a smile*). Thank you for bringing him
back.

GILBERT. Is he your father?

QUEENIE. Father-in-law. A wedding present.

GILBERT. Is he all right?

QUEENIE. I don't think so, do you? He hasn't been right since
the last war. I brought him here to get him away from those
blinking buzz bombs in London – this is my dad's place. But
you lot make such a racket I'm thinking of taking him back
for some peace and quiet.

GILBERT. So, if not Paul Robeson, who him think I was?

QUEENIE (*blushing*). Oh... just someone else I knew. Like you.

GILBERT. An RAF man?

QUEENIE. A coloured chappie – like you.

GILBERT. Oh, I can assure you, madam, there is no other coloured chappie like me.

QUEENIE *suddenly laughs*.

Ah – I make you laugh at last.

QUEENIE. Trying to make me laugh, were you?

GILBERT. Laughter is part of my war effort.

She holds out her hand to GILBERT, *who shakes it*.

QUEENIE. Queenie Bligh. That's Mrs Queenie Bligh to you.

GILBERT. Gilbert Joseph. That's Airman Gilbert Joseph to you.

She laughs again.

QUEENIE. Well, airman. I suppose I'd better ask you in for a cup of tea seeing as you've come all this way.

GILBERT. Regrettably, I will have to decline your kind offer, Mrs Bligh. My Sergeant – Sergeant Bastard – will be awaiting me at the camp.

QUEENIE. Wait a moment then.

QUEENIE *disappears into the house*.

GILBERT (*to audience*). Although having a cup of tea with her was almost worth a court-martial.

QUEENIE *reappears and holds out a pork pie to him*.

QUEENIE. Take this for your walk back.

GILBERT. Oh, no. I can't. Surely your husband would miss it?

QUEENIE. My husband's in Burma. I don't think it'll keep till he gets back.

GILBERT. Sergeant Bastard says we mustn't accept food from the locals because of the shortages.

QUEENIE. And I say, never be polite in a butcher's house.

GILBERT (*taking the pie*). Thank you.

QUEENIE. No, thank you.

GILBERT. Good day, Mrs Bligh.

QUEENIE. Good day, airman.

GILBERT (*to audience*). Man, that pie taste good. Partly because it came from her hand, partly because it was the first thing I had eaten in England that did not look like it had been eaten once before. Why the British boil up everything? How they built an empire when their army march on nothing but mush should be one of the wonders of the world.

A WHITE AMERICAN G.I. *enters and sees* GILBERT.

G.I. 1. Hey you!

GILBERT (*to audience*). So, we arrive at today. This the last day before I am posted further north. A last afternoon off, and I come into this small town in search of some amusement...

GILBERT *starts to walk away from the* G.I. *Two more* WHITE G.I.*s approach from the opposite direction.* GILBERT *steels himself.*

G.I. 1. Hey, you! Salute your superiors, boy!

GILBERT (*to audience*). White American G.I.s – they all over England now. And man, how they hate us black British recruits. Cha, these G.I.s want to kill me more than the Nazis do.

G.I. 2. Salute your superiors!

GILBERT. I don't see any superiors. You a private. You no different from me, man.

G.I. 1 (*squaring up*). What the fuck did you say?

GILBERT *suddenly hears* QUEENIE'*s voice* –

QUEENIE. Airman! Airman! Gilbert!

QUEENIE hurries towards GILBERT, oblivious to the stand-off he's involved in with the G.I.s. The G.I.s back off – surprised and angry. QUEENIE reaches GILBERT.

You haven't seen Arthur, have you?

GILBERT. Don't tell me you lose him again. You have to take more care of the man, Mrs Bligh.

QUEENIE. Don't be cheeky. I only turned my back for a minute. (*Suddenly.*) Oh – there he is.

ARTHUR is walking towards them. He's clutching a bunch of daffodils he's picked.

Arthur, where've you been?

He presents her with the daffodils – shyly, as a lover would. She takes them and smiles, shakes her head.

Oh, you soft beggar.

She kisses him on the cheek. GILBERT is keeping a watchful eye on the G.I.s. They are still standing close by, watching angrily.

GILBERT. Perhaps we should go somewhere else? I could take you for a cup of tea?

QUEENIE. We were going to the pictures. I love the pictures. Fancy joining us, airman?

GILBERT. Why, that would be delightful, Mrs Bligh.

QUEENIE. Good. Come on then.

She slips her arm through GILBERT's. The G.I.s watch with fury. She slips her other arm through ARTHUR's and they walk towards the cinema. GILBERT looks back at the G.I.s and smiles cheekily. One of them draws a finger across his throat by way of a threat.

GILBERT. What's playing?

QUEENIE. *Gone with the Wind.*

GILBERT. Appropriate.

Inside the cinema, the film is about to begin. GILBERT,
QUEENIE *and* ARTHUR *enter and move through the
darkness towards the front. An* USHERETTE *with a torch
intercepts them.*

USHERETTE. Tickets.

QUEENIE *shows her the tickets and the* USHERETTE
shines her torchlight onto some seats at the end of a row.
ARTHUR *and* QUEENIE *proceed to the seats, but as*
GILBERT *goes to pass the* USHERETTE, *she shines the
light in his face and stops him.*

You have to go up the back.

GILBERT (*quietly*). Queenie – she say we have to go up the
back.

USHERETTE (*to* GILBERT). Not her. You.

GILBERT. But we're all together, madam.

USHERETTE. It's the rules.

The USHERETTE *shines her torch along the back row,
revealing a party of* BLACK G.I.*s – not a white face in sight.*

You have to sit with them.

GILBERT. Madam, I am not an American soldier. I am with the
British RAF. No segregation in the British forces.

There are whispers of 'Hush' amongst the audience nearby.
QUEENIE *stands and moves towards them. There are
whispers of 'Sit down!'*

QUEENIE. What's going on?

USHERETTE. Our other customers don't like to sit next to
coloureds.

GILBERT. What other customers? Yanks you mean?

QUEENIE. Look, it'll be all right. He can sit between us...

GILBERT. Wait, Queenie. (*To* USHERETTE.) Madam, in this
country I sit where I like. There is no segregation – no Jim
Crow in this country.

USHERETTE. Who?

GILBERT. Jim Crow.

USHERETTE. Well, if he's coloured he'll have to sit up the back.

GILBERT. This is England, not Alabama.

WHITE G.I. (*loudly*). Sit where you're told, boy!

VOICES. Shh!

GILBERT. None of those coloured men should have to sit at the back.

WHITE G.I. Hey, boy! I said sit where the lady tells you!

QUEENIE. Oh, put a sock in it!

WOMAN. You tell 'em, love! Ruddy loud-mouthed Yanks. Think they own the place!

There are murmurs of agreement.

GILBERT. Come, Queenie – let us sit down.

WHITE G.I. (*standing*). You do as you're told, nigger!

With the use of the word, the tension suddenly intensifies –

BLACK G.I.s. Hey! Who are you calling nigger? (*To* GILBERT.) Stay, man!

QUEENIE (*to* WHITE G.I.). Why don't you shut up?

WHITE G.I. 2. You shut up, nigger-lover!

QUEENIE. Oh, any time over you lot!

WOMAN'S VOICE. Tell 'em, love!

GILBERT. Queenie…

The BLACK G.I.*s now set up a chant –*

BLACK G.I.s. Stay! Stay! Stay!…

USHERETTE (*alarmed*). Look, we don't want any trouble!

WHITE G.I. Fucking uppity niggers! Shut the fuck up!

BLACK G.I.s. Stay! Stay! Stay!…

There is the sound of seats swinging back. The USHERETTE *shines her torch forward. Several* WHITE G.I.*s are making their way down the rows, pushing past* LOCALS.

WHITE G.I.s. Move! Out of the way!

USHERETTE. Stay in your seats!

WOMAN (*to* WHITE G.I.s). Leave them alone, you big bullies!

More and more WHITE G.I.*s start to scramble towards the end of rows as the* BLACK G.I.*s continue to chant and get to their feet.* ARTHUR *is cowering now.*

QUEENIE. It's all right, Arthur! Stay there!

USHERETTE. Go back to your seats!

Suddenly the CINEMA MANAGER *appears on the platform in front of the cinema screen.*

MANAGER (*waving his arms*). Stop the film! Stop the film!

But no one takes any notice. A WHITE G.I. *pushes a* LOCAL *out of the way. Boos and shouts go up.* GILBERT *places himself protectively between* QUEENIE *and the oncoming* WHITE G.I.*s. The film stops.*

Everyone must leave this theatre! I have notified the authorities! Leave this theatre!

The lights in the auditorium suddenly snap on. The film stops and the end of the reel flickers against the white screen. For one second there is silence as everyone takes in the scene – WHITE G.I.*s standing at the front,* BLACK G.I.*s standing at the back – battle lines. A few* LOCALS, *along with* GILBERT, QUEENIE, ARTHUR *and the* USHERETTE *are caught in the middle.*

And in the next second, the fight begins. From either side, WHITE *and* BLACK G.I.*s leaping over seats, charging down aisles and attacking each other.*

A WHITE G.I. *comes at* GILBERT, *punching him in the face.* GILBERT *recovers fast and tackles him. And we are suddenly back where we began.* GILBERT *is getting the better of his opponent, buzzing with adrenalin.*

Suddenly, loud whistles are heard as three AMERICAN
MILITARY POLICEMEN *rush into the auditorium.*

GILBERT. Shit! (*Looking round frantically.*) Queenie, stay
down!

The POLICEMEN *begin to hit the* BLACK G.I.*s with
batons. The whistles are terrifying for* ARTHUR, *who is
cowering with* QUEENIE. *He loses all control. He runs
towards the front of the cinema.* QUEENIE *tries to follow
him, but she is getting pushed around and trapped by the
fighters –*

QUEENIE. Arthur!

Two shots suddenly ring out. One of the MILITARY
POLICEMEN *has fired his gun. People freeze and cower.
The second shot is followed by a woman's scream. Everyone
looks towards where the scream came from – the front of the
cinema. On the platform, a body is lying on the ground.*
GILBERT *realises at once that it's* ARTHUR.

POLICEMAN. Damn it! Stay back! Everyone stay back!

QUEENIE *has started to move towards the platform –*

QUEENIE. Arthur? Arthur?

GILBERT. Queenie!

A MILITARY POLICEMAN *puts an arm across* GILBERT*'s
path.* QUEENIE *reaches the platform.*

POLICEMAN. Stay back!

QUEENIE. But it's Arthur!

She pushes past the POLICEMAN *and reaches* ARTHUR.
She kneels down next to him.

Arthur? It's all right. Come on, now. Come on.

She tries to lift his head. There is blood on his face –

ARTHUR (*faintly*). Queenie…

ARTHUR *dies.*

QUEENIE. Arthur? Arthur? (*To* POLICEMAN.) What have you done? What did you do that for? It's only Arthur!

There are whispers of discontent amongst the LOCALS –

WOMAN. What a bloody disgrace.

POLICEMAN. Everyone out! Move out!

GILBERT (*trying to move towards her*). Queenie!

But a MILITARY POLICEMAN *strikes* GILBERT *with his baton.*

POLICEMAN. No you don't, boy!

GILBERT *is dragged out of the cinema.*

GILBERT. No! No! Queenie! Queenie!

But QUEENIE *doesn't hear. She is weeping over* ARTHUR's *body.*

Scene Four

Winter, 1946.

The war is over. Pathé-style footage of celebrations in Kingston.

On the stage, a festival atmosphere in Kingston. Music playing in the distance, the occasional cheer, laughter. Groups of people passing to and fro in joyous mood.

Enter HORTENSE, *dressed in pristine white – white skirt, blouse, hat and shoes. She is looking for* MICHAEL.

HORTENSE (*quietly*). Michael?

GILBERT *enters with a group of* EX-SERVICEMEN. *They are singing.* GILBERT *is conducting, walking backwards and waving his arms around.*

HORTENSE *sees* GILBERT *and stares. She can only see his back – but she is sure that this is…*

(*To herself.*) Michael.

She goes towards him. When she is close she calls out –

Michael?

GILBERT *doesn't notice her. She reaches out and touches his back –*

Michael?

At the same time, GILBERT *steps back and knocks her over.*

Ah!

GILBERT. Oh, no! Sorry. Sorry. I didn't see you.

HORTENSE. You are not Michael!

GILBERT (*picking her up*). No. I…

HORTENSE. Get your hands off me!.

GILBERT (*letting go*). Whoa! Calm down, nah.

HORTENSE (*looking at the dirt on her clothes*). Look what you have done!

GILBERT *pulls a large handkerchief from his pocket and offers it to her. She snatches it from him and starts to wipe the dirt from her skirt.*

GILBERT. Sorry. It was an accident.

HORTENSE. You are a big, clumsy oaf! You should look where you are going!

GILBERT (*sucking his teeth*). This your idea of a hero's welcome, miss?

HORTENSE *ignores him. She keeps wiping her skirt.*

You want me to do the back for you?

HORTENSE. No, I do not. Go away!

GILBERT (*amused*). Man, you some kind of Spitfire!

GILBERT *starts to walk on.*

HORTENSE. Wait!

GILBERT *stops*.

Are you perchance acquainted with an airman named
Michael Roberts?

GILBERT. Ah – so that why you down here and all dressed up –
you looking for your sweetheart.

HORTENSE. He is not my sweetheart. He's my cousin.

GILBERT (*grinning knowingly*). Oh – your cousin.

HORTENSE. Do you know him or not?

GILBERT. You know his squadron? When you last hear from
him?

HORTENSE. My family had a telegram in April 1944 to say
that he is missing. I am still waiting for him to return.

(*Looking at* GILBERT*'s expression.*) What?

GILBERT. This telegram say 'Missing in action'?

HORTENSE. Yes. I believe that was the phrase it used.

GILBERT. Miss… when a telegram say 'Missing in action', it
generally mean that the person is… Man, no one ever tell
you this? It mean that the person has… passed away.

HORTENSE. This is the British – if they had meant 'passed
away' they would have said 'passed away'. Michael is not
the sort of person to 'pass away'!

Pause. GILBERT *is attracted by her spirit.*

GILBERT. You want to come and get a glass of that lemonade
they serving? You on your own. Looks like I'm on my
own now.

HORTENSE. I do not walk about the streets of Kingston on my
own. I am with my friend, Celia.

GILBERT (*looking round*). She your imaginary friend?

HORTENSE. She is my colleague. And she is over there
somewhere.

GILBERT. Colleague? What you do then?

HORTENSE. We are teachers. Not that it's any of your business.

GILBERT. Man, if my teachers had looked like you, I would have gone to school more often. (*Silence*.) That is a joke. I did very well at school.

HORTENSE. Congratulations.

He smiles, then starts to walk away.

GILBERT. Hope to see you around, Miss Spitfire!

HORTENSE. That is most unlikely.

GILBERT. Why? This a small island, you know!

GILBERT *leaves.* HORTENSE *stands still, trying to process the reality of what* GILBERT *has said about* MICHAEL. *Her friend and colleague,* CELIA LANGLEY, *comes to find her. She is smiling with the joy of the celebration. She notices the mud on* HORTENSE*'s clothes and asks her about it, before taking* HORTENSE *by the arm and leading her off, excitedly, to join the crowds.*

Scene Five

Summer 1947.

Pathé-style footage of Britain's efforts to get back on its feet – rebuilding programmes, etc.

On the stage, an office in the War Office. QUEENIE *is sitting in front of an officer –* CAPTAIN SOAMES *– who is sitting at his desk.*

SOAMES. I've been looking into your husband's case since receiving your letter. Bernard Bligh. Airman. 298 Repair and Salvage Unit. Maintenance Engineer.

Take it there's still been no word?

QUEENIE. No. Last letter I had was around VE Day.

SOAMES. The thing is, Mrs Bligh, according to our records, your husband was demobbed at the end of last year – November 1946.

Pause.

QUEENIE. Right. I see.

SOAMES. Rather late, of course. His unit was one of the unlucky ones. After business with the Japs was wrapped up they got sent into India. Peacekeeping.

QUEENIE. But Bernard didn't sign up for that. He just signed up for the war.

SOAMES. Quite. I'm afraid a lot of the men felt the same.

QUEENIE. So where is he, then, Captain Soames?

SOAMES. Yes. I must say that, very often… when a chap fails to come home after his demob, it's because he…

QUEENIE. Because he doesn't want to come home. Bernard's not like that. Bernard would want to come home.

SOAMES. Oh, I'm sure. I must say, if I were married to you I would want to come home too.

QUEENIE *smiles tightly.*

(*Looking at the file.*) There is one piece of information I could give you. I've rather hesitated to do so…

QUEENIE. What is it?

SOAMES. …but I can see that you're a strong and sensible woman. It seems that your husband served a short spell in military prison towards the end of his time in India.

QUEENIE. Prison?

SOAMES. A two-month sentence.

QUEENIE. What on earth for?

SOAMES. 'Disobeying orders. Losing his weapon.' There are always reasons… stories behind these things. The lead-up to this Partition business was particularly testing. Seems he was a good chap in all other respects.

QUEENIE *stands suddenly.* SOAMES *stands too.*

QUEENIE. What am I supposed to do now? I've got a ruddy great house in Earl's Court that's falling down. I've got bills to pay...

SOAMES. I...

QUEENIE. And what am I? Am I a widow or what? (*Walking to the door.*) Thank you for your time, Captain Soames.

QUEENIE *leaves the office and walks quickly away. She stops for a moment – arrested by a wave of anger and embarrassment – then she walks on.*

Scene Six

Spring, 1948.

A sultry evening in Kingston. Nearby, a political rally is taking place and there is the distant sound of a loudspeaker and a large, volatile crowd. Groups of men run past and there is shouting close by.

CELIA *and* HORTENSE *walk arm in arm to a meeting place.* HORTENSE, *perfectly dressed, is ill at ease.* CELIA *is excited.*

CELIA. I am so excited that you will meet my RAF man at last.

HORTENSE. We shouldn't stay here, Celia. There's another of those rallies happening. People were injured yesterday.

CELIA. Hortense, my honey, you worry too much. I'm sure my RAF man will ask me again if I will go to England with him. What do you think of that? He served there in the war. Have I told you that before?

HORTENSE. Once or twice.

CELIA. In England I will have a big house with a bell on the front door, and I will ring the bell – 'Ding-a-ling. Ding-a-ling'. What do you think of that, Hortense?

HORTENSE. My, my, Celia Langley.

CELIA. In England, I will have a lace tablecloth and fine bone-china teacups. What do you think of that, Hortense?

HORTENSE. I think it is a pleasant dream for you, Celia.

CELIA. It is not just a dream.

HORTENSE. I don't see how you can go to England – given your particular circumstances.

GILBERT enters. He looks shabby, down-at-heel, but he is trying to stay cheerful.

CELIA. Oh, look – there he is! (*To* HORTENSE.) Is my hair still neat?

HORTENSE. Hair like yours will never be neat. But it will suffice.

CELIA. Gilbert!

He comes to her and kisses her, but then his eyes fall on HORTENSE.

GILBERT (*to* HORTENSE). Well, hello again.

HORTENSE (*stopping*). You.

CELIA (*puzzled*). Have you two met?

GILBERT (*to* CELIA). Don't tell me this the friend you always talking to me about? Why you not tell me it little Miss Spitfire? (*To* HORTENSE.) You found your cousin yet?

CELIA. What cousin? What are you two talking about?

GILBERT. I met her on my first day home. I picked her up.

HORTENSE. You knocked me down.

CELIA (*to* GILBERT). You picked her up? (*To* HORTENSE.) He picked you up?

ELWOOD is walking past with a group of men, heading towards the rally. He sees GILBERT –

ELWOOD. Gilbert, you coming to the rally? What's this? You got two women on the go and you keeping them both to yourself?

HORTENSE. I am not 'on the go'.

ELWOOD *kisses* CELIA*'s hand. She giggles*.

GILBERT. This Celia's friend – Miss Spitfire.

CELIA (*laughing*). Gilbert! This is my very best friend, Hortense.

GILBERT. She a bit ferocious.

ELWOOD. You coming to the rally?

GILBERT. Do I look like I'm coming to the rally?

CELIA. Are you going to hear Mr Bustamante speak?

ELWOOD. When Busta speak I'm always there. (*Indicating* GILBERT.) Not like him. He's not interested in his country's independence. He prefer to go licky-licky to the British.

GILBERT (*sharply*). There's no licky-licky about it. There's way more opportunities in England…

ELWOOD. Dirty work! What job is it they offer you when you finish your soldier-boying? Baking. Where the big promise of university?

GILBERT. They just sorting themselves out nah.

ELWOOD. Cha!

GILBERT. Even baking got to be better than standing in line for handouts. Better than the job we did last week. (*To* CELIA.) We spend last week in a field burying the corpses of dead cattle. Diseased cattle. That the only work we could get. That just about sum up this island right now.

ELWOOD. You got to have a likkle faith. When we in charge of Jamaica…

GILBERT. You will work for a black man instead of a white man! You a dreamer, Elwood!

ELWOOD. And you not?!

The argument has grown heated. At the rally, shots are being fired into the air.

CELIA. If you two boys were in my class I would tell you off for squabbling. Wouldn't I, Hortense?

ELWOOD (*to* HORTENSE). You want to come to the rally with me? Listen to Busta speak some sense?

HORTENSE. I do not attend public rallies.

ELWOOD. I lift you high-high on my shoulders so you can see above the crowd.

ELWOOD *goes to put his hands around* HORTENSE's *waist. She slaps them off.* CELIA *laughs.*

HORTENSE (*fixing her with a stare*). You think this is funny, Celia?

CELIA. Sorry. But it is quite funny.

ELWOOD (*leaving*). Later, man. We make a nice foursome!

ELWOOD *goes after his friends.* GILBERT *fights off his annoyance. He scoffs and smiles.*

GILBERT (*imitating* ELWOOD). 'When Busta speak, I'm always there.' Only a fool would stay on this island right now.

CELIA. Oh, I agree, Gilbert.

GILBERT. England is where the future lies.

CELIA *leans into him and wraps her arms around his neck.*

CELIA. Gilbert, tell Hortense about all the things you saw in England.

GILBERT. Oh, there are so many fine sights in England. Let me ask you this one question – you ever see a picture of the House of Parliament in London? When you stand there before it, it look to all the world like a fairytale castle. You think dragons will come out and breathe fire on you.

CELIA. Oh, I would like to see that. Wouldn't you, Hortense?

HORTENSE (*quietly*). Yes. Yes, I would.

GILBERT. Then come to England with me, Celia.

CELIA. Oh, Gilbert. What do you think – shall I go, Hortense?

GILBERT. Why not? As soon as I have saved up the money we will get on a boat.

CELIA. But what about my class? I have a job, you know?

GILBERT. Your friend here can teach your class for you.

CELIA *giggles*.

What do you say? Will you come, Celia?

CELIA. Yes, Gilbert. I shall go.

GILBERT. Good. Good! Hortense will take care of everything. She will stay here and write to us of the rallies, and the fights and the blights and the earthquakes...

CELIA. And the hurricanes.

GILBERT.... while we sip tea and search for the dragons in the House of Parliament.

CELIA. Oh, poor Hortense! I feel sorry for you.

Silence. HORTENSE *turns to look at the audience – an ominous look.*

HORTENSE. But, Celia, what about your mother? Am I to look after her too?

The playful light in CELIA*'s eyes goes out.*

GILBERT. Bring your mother. We will row with her on the Thames. (*Looking at* CELIA*'s expression.*) Or leave her. What is wrong with your mother?

HORTENSE. Surely she has told you? Oh, dear. Celia's mother is not at all well. In fact, you might have seen her about the town. She is the one who wears the child's party dress and the orange wig. Sometimes she grabs people in the street and tries to kiss them. Poor Celia is the only one who can control her. Because you see, Celia's mother, unfortunately, is completely mad.

Silence.

GILBERT. I'm sorry to hear that about your mother.

HORTENSE. Yes, I am also sorry for her. Because it is quite impossible that Celia could leave her – being an only child, as well.

Silence.

CELIA. May I speak to you alone for a moment, Hortense?

HORTENSE. Why yes, Celia.

CELIA *walks some distance away.* HORTENSE *follows her.*

HORTENSE. I thought it would be better if he...

CELIA *swings round and hits* HORTENSE *in the face.* HORTENSE *staggers and falls to the ground.* CELIA *walks off into the night.*

Celia! (*Clasping her mouth in pain.*) Celia!

HORTENSE *stays on stage as –*

Scene Seven

The house in Earl's Court. The sitting room looks dingy and neglected. The only sign of life is a teapot and a cup on a table.

MICHAEL (*off*). Hello?!

MICHAEL *enters. He is wearing a smart three-piece suit and a hat. He has a coat slung over his shoulder and carries a small case in his hand.*

Hello?

He puts the case down. QUEENIE *enters from the direction of the kitchen. She is carrying a large scuttle full of coal. She sees* MICHAEL *and gasps –*

QUEENIE. Ah!

MICHAEL. Sorry. The front door was open. I called out.

QUEENIE. Sergeant Michael Roberts.

MICHAEL. Just Michael Roberts now.

Pause. They stare at one another. QUEENIE *looks worn out – sad, somehow.*

QUEENIE. Nice suit.

MICHAEL. Thank you. (*Of the coal scuttle.*) You want a hand with that?

QUEENIE. Oh. No. Don't worry.

She carries it to the fireplace and puts it down. She remembers how unglamorous she looks – her apron on, her hair covered in a scarf. She pulls the scarf off her head, embarrassed.

I wasn't expecting anyone.

MICHAEL. I'm glad to find you still live here. You on your own? Where's Arthur?

QUEENIE. That's a long story. But he's dead.

MICHAEL. Ah, no. I'm sorry to hear that. I was looking forward to playing another hand of cards with him. I was hoping he would show me how he cheated me out of all my money that night.

QUEENIE (*smiling*). There was more to Arthur than met the eye.

MICHAEL. There was. What about your husband?

QUEENIE. Another long story. He's not back.

Pause. MICHAEL *nods.*

MICHAEL. I was hoping… Would it be possible for me to stay the night?

QUEENIE. Yes. Yes, it would. I think I can accommodate you. In fact, you can take your pick of rooms.

MICHAEL. Thank you. I'm sailing to Canada tomorrow, so I won't be under your feet for long.

QUEENIE (*stunned*). Blimey. Canada.

MICHAEL. I did my training there. Huge skies. Huge opportunities. I can't wait to get back.

QUEENIE *turns away to cover her disappointment. She starts to take her apron off but her fingers are shaking and she can't undo the ties.* MICHAEL *moves towards her to help. Their proximity is electrifying. Their fingers brush against one another's accidentally. Then* QUEENIE *stands still, her heart pounding, and waits as he undoes the knot. He hands her the apron. There's a moment of quiet intensity.*

QUEENIE. Sit down.

He does so. She sits down too, some distance away. They look at each.

I've been quite worried about you, actually.

MICHAEL. Oh?

QUEENIE. Only I bumped into Franny last year and she told me about Kip. And I thought perhaps…

MICHAEL. No. I was the lucky one – had a soft landing. Sprained ankle, that's all. Kip went down with the plane. Ginger… We used our parachutes but Ginger's caught fire.

QUEENIE. I'm sorry. They were really nice lads.

MICHAEL. They were.

Pause.

QUEENIE. Where were you? I mean… where did you… land?

MICHAEL. Over France. I landed in a field. Managed to hide. Dug turnips from the soil with my hands and eat them raw. (*Smiling.*) Then the farmer found me. Couldn't believe his eyes – a black man in the middle of his field. He hid me for months. Then he handed me over to the Americans. They passed me on to the British.

QUEENIE. Thank God.

MICHAEL. Funny – I'd had a bad feeling about that mission. I'd lost my good-luck charm. Kip said I could share his. Must have taken more than my share of the luck.

QUEENIE *stands and takes something from her pocket – a wallet. She holds it out to* MICHAEL.

QUEENIE. It wasn't in here, was it??

MICHAEL is staring at it, emotion visible in his eyes.

Your wallet. I found it on the stairs after you'd left. I tried coming after you but you were all long gone.

He takes it from her as though it is a precious relic. She sits down next to him and watches as he opens it and takes out a photograph from inside. He stares at it, struggling to contain his emotions.

Is the photo of your family? I hope you don't mind – I looked inside in case there was an address. Sweet little girl. Is she your sister?

MICHAEL. I lost my family. In a hurricane.

He puts the photo back in the wallet.

This was my good-luck charm. (*Looking deeply into her eyes.*) You kept it.

QUEENIE. Yes. I hoped you might come back.

MICHAEL (*taking this in*). You kept it in your pocket.

QUEENIE*'s heart is beating fast. She pushes her hair away from her face, leaving a smudge of coal dust on her cheek.* MICHAEL *smiles.*

QUEENIE. What's funny?

He reaches for her hand and holds it in his. He turns it over.

MICHAEL. Your palms are blacker than mine.

Their hands intertwine. They kiss passionately. They slide from the chairs and onto their knees, kissing.

GILBERT *enters. He is holding a flyer in his hand – it is advertising the sailing of the* Empire Windrush *to England. He is reading it.* HORTENSE *goes to him.*

GILBERT. Ah. Miss Spitfire. You seen this? The *Empire Windrush*, sailing for England. Two months' time. Man, I wish I could be on that ship.

HORTENSE. Perhaps you could be.

GILBERT. You seen how much it cost? Twenty-eight pounds and ten shillings. That's twenty-eight pounds and ten shillings I haven't got.

HORTENSE. I will lend you the money.

GILBERT. What, sorry?

She doesn't reply.

I don't understand.

HORTENSE. Prudence. Something my uncle taught me. A little of my wages every week.

You can pay me back.

GILBERT. Oh, I surely would. What I don't understand, is why you would lend me the money?

HORTENSE. So you can go to England. I will lend you the money, we will be married and you can send for me to come to England when you have a place for me to live.

GILBERT. Whoa! Just say that again because I think me ears playing a trick on me.

HORTENSE. A single woman cannot travel on her own – it would not be respectable. But a married woman might go anywhere she pleases. Marry me, and go to England.

In her bedroom in Earl's Court, QUEENIE *and* MICHAEL *are making love.*

QUEENIE (*to audience and herself*). This isn't me. Mrs Queenie Bligh isn't even here. This woman is a beauty. He can't get enough of her. This woman is as sexy as a starlet on the silver screen. This woman is desirable, wild with desire, clawing his back and crying out till his mouth fills hers with his eager tongue. This isn't me. Mrs Queenie Bligh works out what's for dinner during conjugal relations with her husband. But this woman... this woman pants and thrusts and bites and yelps. This woman is far, far gone. Live. Electric. Bright. Bright. Bright.

GILBERT *leaves* HORTENSE *and goes to stand alone.*

GILBERT (*to audience and himself*). This is a tough one. Man, this woman don't even like me as far as I can tell. My face seem to distress her, my jokes confuse her. She surely thinks she's better than me. Oh, she's pretty – even her lips might be sweet if they were not always pinched up. How this woman learn to sneer so? But *England*.

HORTENSE (*to audience and herself*). I'm sorry. I'm sorry, Celia… I cannot be the fool who is left behind again. It is better that I go to England. England will give me a fine welcome because of my pale pale skin and my education. England is my golden life.

In the bedroom in Earl's Court, MICHAEL finishes getting dressed. QUEENIE, half-dressed, is sitting on the side of the bed, staring at the floor.

GILBERT (*to audience and himself*). I'm done with this small island. I seen too much of the world now. I stay here, I become one of those big-talk men, small coins jangling in my ragged pockets even as I tell my tales. How I ever be a lawyer if I stay here? Man, there is no decision to make. But this is not what I imagine. This…

Tears of broken pride gather in his eyes and he turns away.

HORTENSE (*to audience and herself*). In England I will have a smart front door and I will ring the bell – ding-a-ling, ding-a-ling. I will be a teacher, greeted with manners and respect. And no one… no one will feel sorry for I.

In Earl's Court, MICHAEL goes to QUEENIE, lifts her face to his and kisses her profoundly. There are tears in her eyes. Then he puts on his hat and slings his coat over his shoulder. He picks up his suitcase. They look at each other and smile. MICHAEL leaves. QUEENIE is still for a moment, then she buries her face in her hands and weeps.

GILBERT *gathers himself together and reaches a decision –*

GILBERT (*to audience and himself*). No. Come, Gilbert. This woman has guessed your price, and it is the price of a ticket to England.

Scene Eight

May 28th, 1948. Empire Day.

Kingston Docks. The Empire Windrush *is preparing to sail.*

HORTENSE *and* GILBERT, *beautifully dressed, have been married.* ELWOOD *takes a photograph of them – standing side by side, arm in arm, dignified, unsmiling. Next to* GILBERT *is a small suitcase of his belongings.*

ELWOOD *leaves. Excitement increases around* GILBERT *and* HORTENSE, *as men prepare to board the ship and families gather to wave the men off.*

HORTENSE. You won't get to England forgetting all about me and leave me here?

GILBERT. Of course not. As soon as I have somewhere to stay I'll write to you. Hortense, can I have a kiss nah? Just one? We married after all.

HORTENSE *allows* GILBERT *to kiss her on the cheek – but as soon as he tries to put his arms around her, she moves them off.* GILBERT *accepts this. He watches her with a hint of affection as she smooths the fabric of her white coat.*

HORTENSE. There may be women who will turn your head in England.

GILBERT. You jealous already?

HORTENSE. No. But you must always remember what you have promised.

GILBERT. We have a deal, Hortense. Look – (*Saluting.*) I give you my RAF salute. That is the salute of a gentleman.

He leaves to join the ship.

Goodbye! I see you soon, Hortense!

On the deck of the Windrush, GILBERT *stands amongst the other men, waving to* HORTENSE, *as the ship starts to sail.*

On the dock, HORTENSE *waves to* GILBERT.

HORTENSE. Send for me! Don't forget! Send for me! (*To herself.*) Please...

In Earl's Court, QUEENIE *lifts her blouse with trembling hands and looks down at her tummy – there is a small but unmistakeable bump. She is pregnant.*

QUEENIE. Oh, Queenie. What have you done?

ACT TWO

Scene One

A grey, starkly realistic world.

A small room at the top of QUEENIE*'s house in Earl's Court.*
A single bed, a small table and two chairs – one of which has
a broken leg and rests on an old book. There is a gas fire and an
armchair. A suit hangs on a hanger on the back of the door.
In one corner there is a gas ring, a sink and a kettle. A very
small window looks out onto rooftops. It is a late afternoon in
November and the sky is already growing dim.

GILBERT, *fully-dressed, is asleep on the bed. Downstairs, the*
front-door bell rings. After a moment it rings again. GILBERT
suddenly sits up.

GILBERT. Oh, no.

He checks his watch.

No! No, no, no!

The bell rings again as GILBERT *frantically pulls on his*
shoes and fastens the loose buttons on his shirt.

No!

Female voices can be heard in the hall now. GILBERT
rushes from the room, tripping over his not-quite-done-up
shoelaces, and we hear the sound of him running down the
stairs. We hear his voice joining those of the others, loud at
first and then quiet. We hear a rat running over the roof of
the room, scratching and scurrying.

Footsteps approach on the stairs.

(*Off.*) Not much further now.

More footsteps. GILBERT *appears in the doorway and holds*
the door open for HORTENSE *to enter. She is dressed in*
a pristine white coat with the white hat and gloves she wore

*for her wedding. She has a handbag over her arm. She is
a little breathless.*

Here we are.

HORTENSE *stands in the doorway, taking in the room.
She is disorientated, shocked, inwardly afraid, but she is
determined to cover it.* GILBERT *rushes to pull the covers
over the unmade bed – a move which does not escape*
HORTENSE*'s notice. He looks at her, smiling nervously.
She swallows.*

HORTENSE. Well. Show me the rest.

She looks at him and he stares at her.

Show me the rest, nah. I am tired from the long, long
journey. The other rooms, Gilbert. The ones you say you so
busy making nice for me that you forget to come and meet
me at the dock.

GILBERT. But… this is it.

HORTENSE. I beg your pardon?

GILBERT. This is it. This is the room I am living.

HORTENSE *stares around at the room again in shocked
silence.*

HORTENSE. Just this?

*She suddenly has to sit down on the edge of a chair so that
her legs don't give way.* GILBERT *swings his arms as
though to suggest how spacious the room is.*

GILBERT. Yes. This is it.

HORTENSE. Just this?

GILBERT. What you expect? Yes, just this. There has been a war.
Houses bombed. I know plenty people live worse than this.

Footsteps are heard on the stairs.

QUEENIE (*off*). Gilbert!

HORTENSE *stands as* QUEENIE *enters. She is flushed and
breathless. She looks a little rounder, but is not obviously
pregnant.*

Sorry. You're going to have to move that trunk, you know? You can't just leave it by the steps.

GILBERT. Course. I come nah.

QUEENIE. I would say someone'll make off with it except it's that bloody heavy.

GILBERT *glances at* HORTENSE*'s shocked face.*

GILBERT. I come nah. I get Winston to help me.

QUEENIE. Oh, I don't think that's Winston in his room. I think it's Kenneth. (*To* HORTENSE.) They're twins, you see. But the one who's in there now just looked up my skirt so I'm pretty sure it's Kenneth.

GILBERT. Right. I get Kenneth to help me then. (*To* HORTENSE.) I won't be long.

GILBERT *leaves.* QUEENIE *smiles at* HORTENSE. *She sits down on the edge of the bed – needing a moment's rest.* HORTENSE *is confused – why is this woman making herself at home in her room?*

QUEENIE. So you're Gilbert's wife. What's your name again?

HORTENSE. Hortense.

QUEENIE. Hortense. Funny name. My name's Mrs Bligh, but you can call me Queenie if you like? Everyone here does. Would you like that?

HORTENSE *hesitates to reply.*

Cat got your tongue?

HORTENSE. What cat?

QUEENIE. Oh. No, it's just an expression. It means you're not saying much. Don't worry, you'll soon pick up English.

He didn't come to meet you then? Men, eh? I'm sure he meant to. He told me he was going to. So how long have you and Gilbert been married? (*Loudly and slowly.*) How... long... have...?

HORTENSE. Gilbert and I have been married for six and a half months.

QUEENIE. Six? Six months?

HORTENSE. That is what I said.

QUEENIE. What – altogether? But Gilbert's been here for about four. Ah. You're newlyweds then. Sweet.

HORTENSE. I suppose so.

QUEENIE. Did you say 'I suppose so'? You don't sound too pleased about it.

There sounds of footsteps on the stairs now and some bumping and cursing.

Oh, no, what are they doing?

QUEENIE *leaves.*

(*Off.*) You know that bannister's dodgy, don't you?

Watch out for the paintwork!

HORTENSE *goes into the kitchen area. She stares at the dirty sink. She runs a finger of her white glove along the window pane and it turns black. She stares back at the room in disbelief.*

KENNETH *bursts through the door holding one end of* HORTENSE*'s trunk.* GILBERT *follows him in with the other. They are straining under the weight of it.*

KENNETH (*to* HORTENSE). Man, what you got in here? Your mother?

HORTENSE. You may place it in that corner and please be careful.

KENNETH *looks at* GILBERT *and they drop the trunk where they stand.*

Careful! That is a very expensive trunk!

KENNETH *is staring at* HORTENSE. *He is a shifty-looking, scruffy young man.*

GILBERT. Kenneth, this is Hortense. My wife.

HORTENSE. How do you do?

KENNETH. What part of the island you from?

HORTENSE. I have been living in Kingston but...

KENNETH. What your name before you marry him?

HORTENSE. My name was Roberts...

KENNETH. What ship you come on?

HORTENSE. I...

KENNETH. You meet a man on the ship from Buff Bay? His name Clinton.

HORTENSE. No, I...

KENNETH. So what you got in the trunk? Apart from your mother.

KENNETH *chuckles at his own joke*.

HORTENSE. I have my possessions in that trunk...

KENNETH. Any rum? Mango? Guava? Tell me you got guava. Guava fetch a good price right now. I know one of the boys give me half his wage to place him tongue in a guava.

HORTENSE *is looking at him with disdain*.

GILBERT. Thank you for your help, Kenneth.

KENNETH. What? Surely you got something for me?

GILBERT. I tell you what – you can take a shilling off the six shilling you already owe me.

KENNETH *sucks his teeth*.

KENNETH (*to* HORTENSE). You sure you haven't got any rum, nah? (*To* GILBERT.) Cha, why don't you tell her to bring some rum with her?

GILBERT. Goodbye, Kenneth.

KENNETH. You goin', man?

GILBERT *signals that he wants to be alone with* HORTENSE *– staring at* HORTENSE *and then shifting his eyes towards the door repeatedly.*

Oh. (*Nodding and grinning.*) Oh. I must be gone. Leave you two alone. Five months – that a long time.

He chuckles again – pleased with himself, and then he leaves. His footsteps are heard going down the stairs.

HORTENSE. That man is your friend?

GILBERT. Why you no sit down nah?

HORTENSE. Why would you choose such a friend?

GILBERT. Any boy from back home a friend here, believe me.

Take off your coat. The fire is on so… Oh – it gone out. I have to put more money in the meter. (*Checking his pockets.*) Where I put that shilling?

(*Searching through the bedcovers.*) Had it put aside special.

HORTENSE. You keep your money in the bed?

GILBERT. No. But when I was sleeping it must have fallen out me pocket…

HORTENSE. Oh. So you were sleeping then?

GILBERT *stops still – caught out.*

GILBERT. No. I just lie for a minute and…

HORTENSE. So that why you no there to meet me.

GILBERT. No. I came but…

HORTENSE. What is it you write in your letter? 'I will be at the dockside to meet you. You will see me there, jumping and waving and calling your name with longing in my tone.'

GILBERT. Hortense, Hortense, let me tell you. I worked a shift at the post office last night. In the morning I went straight to the dock but there was no ship. So they tell me to come back later when the ship will arrive. So I go home to take the opportunity of fixing the place up nice for you…

HORTENSE. Oh, yes. See how nice it is.

GILBERT. And I just lie for a minute and I fall asleep. I so tired. And next thing I know you are ringing the bell and…

HORTENSE. Do you know what a fool I feel waiting on that dock? Waiting and waiting…

GILBERT. I know…

HORTENSE. And everyone else is meeting people or going off in little twos and threes…

GILBERT. I'm sorry…

HORTENSE. And then the taxi driver could not understand what I am saying when I tell him this address, and I begin to wonder if this place even…

GILBERT. Sorry. I'm sorry. Hortense, I am glad you are here. Man, I look forward to this day so long.

HORTENSE (*unconvinced*). Really?

GILBERT. Yes! Of course. I have my wife with me at last.

HORTENSE *is silent.* GILBERT *spots the coin on the floor and picks it up sheepishly.*

Let me sort the fire out nah. Let me show you how to put the money in the meter.

HORTENSE. You think I don't know how to put money into a meter?

GILBERT *tries to put the coin in the meter but it jams. He kicks the meter, but still it does not go in.* HORTENSE *watches with disdain as he stands back and kicks the meter again. The coin goes in.* HORTENSE *turns away and sucks her teeth.* GILBERT *lights the fire.*

GILBERT. You wan' a cup of tea? I'll make you a nice cup of English tea. Yes?

She assents with the slightest of nods. GILBERT *goes into the kitchen area and puts the kettle on.*

Take off your coat nah.

HORTENSE *takes off her coat reluctantly. She leaves her hat and gloves on. She is wearing the white dress which she wore for the wedding.* GILBERT *goes to her and takes her coat from her. He hangs it over the suit – his wedding suit – on the back of the door.* HORTENSE *is still taking in the room.*

HORTENSE. Only one bed.

GILBERT. Yes. But nights here very cold, yah know? And we…

HORTENSE. At least you will have a chair to sleep on.

GILBERT *almost protests but decides not to.* HORTENSE *sits down.*

Who is that woman downstairs?

GILBERT. Queenie. She own the house. She is the landlady.

HORTENSE. She married?

GILBERT. Her husband lost in the war.

HORTENSE. She on her own?

GILBERT. Yes.

HORTENSE. You friendly with her?

GILBERT *freezes and thinks for a moment before answering.*

GILBERT. I knew her during the war. She was kind to me. Lucky I remember her address. Lucky she still here. Places hard to come by, especially for coloured boys.

HORTENSE. She seem to know all your business.

GILBERT. What? No. She just friendly.

HORTENSE. Who else live in this house?

GILBERT. Winston. Him exactly like Kenneth but honest. And a white woman called Jean. You won't see her much. She work nights.

HORTENSE. She a nurse?

GILBERT. Something like that. Come – I show you how to use the gas ring. It only small but it surprising what you can cook up on it.

HORTENSE. I will cook in the kitchen.

Pause.

GILBERT. This is the kitchen.

HORTENSE. Where?

GILBERT. This ring. This sink. This is the kitchen.

HORTENSE. Just this? There is no kitchen down the stairs?

GILBERT. Not for us to use. This is the kitchen. (*Pointing to the table and chairs*.) That is the dining room. I thought you...

HORTENSE, aghast, takes this in.

HORTENSE. And what about the lavatory? Tell me we have our own lavatory.

GILBERT. No. The lavatory is on the ground floor. It's a shared lavatory.

HORTENSE. Do you mean to tell me, that every time I need the lavatory, I must go all the way down those stairs and then come all the way back up again?

GILBERT. Yes. (*Suddenly.*) No! No –

Excited, he goes to the bed and pulls a potty out from underneath.

Sometimes I use this.

He shows it to her. But the potty is full and some of the contents slop over the side. HORTENSE jumps back in disgust.

Oh!

HORTENSE. Disgusting! What are you doing?!

GILBERT. Sorry! I forgot it was... Oh, no...

HORTENSE. This place is disgusting! How you bring me here?!

GILBERT. Hush!

HORTENSE. I caan believe you bring me all this way for a place like this! You tell me you have somewhere nice to live. You want me to live like this?!

GILBERT (*moving towards her and forgetting the potty*). Hush nah. No need to tell the whole...

HORTENSE. Get it away from me! I caan believe you bring me here. You live like an animal!

GILBERT. You should see the place I was living when I first arrived – crammed into one room with eight other boys, lying in each other's sweat...

HORTENSE. I don't want to know...

GILBERT. You should see the number of doors I knock on, the faces that cloud at the sight of me. 'The room has gone. The room has gone.' That if they even deign to speak to me. 'If it was just me I'd let you have it, but it's my husband you see, it's my wife you see, it's the neighbours you see, there are *children* in this house you see?'

GILBERT *strides into the kitchen. He throws the contents of the potty into the basin and slams the potty down. There is silence for a moment.*

HORTENSE. What did you just do? There are cups in that basin. You tell me... you tell me you wash your cups in the same place you throw your doings?

GILBERT. No. No, I don't. I take it down to the toilet. But you are getting me so...

HORTENSE. You wash in filth! This place is disgusting! You make me come here to live like an animal!

GILBERT. Yes! Yes! And you know what else, Little Miss Stick-up-your-nose-in-the-air, you will have to wash your plate, your vegetable and your backside in that basin too. This room is where you will sleep, eat, cook, dress and write your mummy to tell her how the Mother Country is so fine. And let me tell you this one thing – you are lucky!

Scene Two

The following morning. The living room in QUEENIE's *house. A small table and chairs. A small sofa and an armchair. An occasional table, a sideboard, a large radio. A fireplace with a coal scuttle. The morning news is on the radio.*

Footsteps in the hall. A short knock on the door of the room. QUEENIE *enters from the kitchen, wiping her hands on her apron.*

MISS TODD (*off*). Mrs Bligh!

QUEENIE. Oh, no.

> QUEENIE *hesitates. For a moment she thinks she won't open the door. There is another knock.*

MISS TODD (*off*). Mrs Bligh!

> QUEENIE *strides to the door and opens it. Her next-door neighbour,* MISS TODD (*white, sixties, genteel*) *is standing with her hand raised as though about to knock again.*

Ah. You *are* here. One of them let me in.

QUEENIE. Gilbert. On his way to work at the post office. Works very hard does Gilbert.

MISS TODD. I need to have a word with you, Mrs Bligh...

QUEENIE. Actually, Miss Todd, I was just finishing my breakfast so...

> MISS TODD *enters the room. She glances round, disdainfully, then looks at* QUEENIE *and smiles forcefully.*

MISS TODD. How has the chimney been since I had it swept?

QUEENIE. Much better, thank you.

MISS TODD. Good. And no more pigeons in the roof?

QUEENIE. No.

MISS TODD. That's what neighbours are for. We have to look after one another, don't we? Think about each other.

QUEENIE. So what can I do for you, Miss Todd?

MISS TODD. It's about your paying guests.

QUEENIE. Oh? Really? Again?

MISS TODD. We couldn't help but notice that another one arrived yesterday. A female.

QUEENIE. That's Gilbert's wife. She's come to join him. Sweet, isn't it?

MISS TODD. Mrs Bligh…

QUEENIE. Queenie.

MISS TODD. I'm not sure you quite understand the amount of unease this is causing amongst your neighbours. And you're not the only one taking them in now. There are two households further along which have started to follow your example…

QUEENIE. They're just lodgers like anyone else. And I need the money coming in so…

MISS TODD. I don't blame *you*, of course. It's the Government who are to blame. That new 'National Health Service'. Giving things away at our expense! It's the teeth and glasses that are bringing them here. And now that they are here we shall have a struggle to get rid of them. Short-sighted.

QUEENIE. Are they? I hadn't noticed any of them being especially…

MISS TODD. The Government policy, I mean.

QUEENIE. Oh.

Pause. MISS TODD *stares at her – she knows she's being facetious.*

MISS TODD. Do you know that Mr and Mrs Smith at number seven are being forced out because of this?

QUEENIE. I know that they're moving. Bromley, isn't it?

MISS TODD. That house has been in her family for generations. She cried when she told me they have to leave. But her husband just won't have it. He has two young daughters to think about. He doesn't want them being... eyed up by these coons every time they step out on the street...

QUEENIE. I'm quite sure none of my lodgers would...

MISS TODD. He's just back from fighting a war and now he feels like a stranger in his own country. 'What was it all for?' That's what he said to me.

QUEENIE. Crikey. Anyone would think I was renting rooms to the Gestapo.

Pause.

MISS TODD. I'm quite sure that Mr Bligh would not approve of this situation...

QUEENIE. Well, he's not here, is he? And if he was, I wouldn't be so desperate for the money. (*Moving towards the door.*) I really do want to get on now, Miss Todd.

MISS TODD (*suddenly and forcefully*). There was a very unpleasant incident yesterday morning involving my sister Alice. She was walking home from the shops with a heavy bag, when two of them – two of those darkie women came walking towards her. And my sister, *my sister* was made to step off the pavement and walk into the road to get by. They had no intention whatsoever of letting her pass undisturbed.

So I would like you to make it very clear to your lodgers, that, as they are guests in this country, it should be they who step off the pavement when an English person approaches.

HORTENSE *appears in the doorway, knocking gently on the open door.*

QUEENIE. Oh. Well, here's one of them now. Why don't you tell her yourself?

Miss Todd was just saying, Hortense, that you need to step into the road if you see her sister coming.

MISS TODD. I didn't...

QUEENIE. She needs a lot of room to get past.

HORTENSE *looks at her and at* MISS TODD, *bewildered.*

MISS TODD (*raising herself up*). I hope you will consider what I've said.

QUEENIE. Oh, certainly.

MISS TODD. Good day.

> MISS TODD *moves past* HORTENSE, *and leaves. The front door is heard closing.* QUEENIE *is flushed and a little breathless.*

QUEENIE (*quietly*). Ridiculous woman.

> Sorry, Hortense – what can I do for you? Come in.

HORTENSE. No. It's...

QUEENIE. No, please. Please.

> HORTENSE *moves into the room.*

> Did you sleep well? Quite cosy up there, isn't it? Heat rises, isn't that what they say?

HORTENSE. I was wondering if you have another basin I can have a use of?

QUEENIE. A what?

HORTENSE. A basin.

QUEENIE. Sorry. A bees what?

HORTENSE. A basin. A sort of... bucket... to put in the sink. For washing and...

QUEENIE. Oh! A basin.

HORTENSE. Yes.

QUEENIE. But there's one up there, isn't there?

HORTENSE. Yes, but I will be needing three of them. One for washing. One for the vegetable...

QUEENIE. No. No, you just use the same one. You don't need *three*. Just keep it clean.

> Do you want me to show you how to keep it clean?

HORTENSE. I know how to keep things clean.

QUEENIE. Yes. I'm sure. I didn't mean... Yes. So what are you going to do today?

HORTENSE. I will go to the shops.

QUEENIE. Good idea. I'll come with you if you like?

HORTENSE. No, thank you.

QUEENIE. I will. It's no trouble. Do you have shops where you come from?

HORTENSE. Yes.

QUEENIE. We have everything here. Grocers. Butchers. Bakers – they sell bread. You'll have to use your ration book. It's not difficult. I'll show you.

HORTENSE. No. Thank you.

QUEENIE. I don't mind being seen on the street with you. I'm not like some.

HORTENSE (*puzzled*). I...

QUEENIE. To be honest, I'd be glad of the company. It's ages since I had a proper woman to chat with.

Pause.

Shall we say half an hour then?

HORTENSE. Very well.

QUEENIE. Good. Just knock on the door when you're ready.

HORTENSE *hesitates*.

HORTENSE. I wondered if you might tell me where I can find the department in charge of education?

QUEENIE. Education, did you say? Ah – do you want to have English lessons? I'm not quite sure where it is but I'm sure I can find out.

Pause.

HORTENSE. Thank you.

QUEENIE. Pleasure.

HORTENSE leaves. QUEENIE follows her to the door and closes it behind her. Then she locks it. She breathes out heavily. She takes out a handkerchief and wipes the moisture from her brow. She lifts her apron and her blouse to reveal some tight binding around her tummy. She undoes the binding, sighing with the relief. She is very pregnant. She leans on the table and takes deep, long breaths as her baby kicks inside her.

Scene Three

The same morning. King's Cross Station. At a back entrance, GILBERT has arrived to collect newly arrived bags of mail. He's not sure where to find them. A FOREMAN (white) approaches him –

FOREMAN. Oi, you!

GILBERT. Yes?

FOREMAN. What you doing?

GILBERT. I'm on my own today. Bert's sick so…

FOREMAN. Oh, yes? Caught something, has he? There's a surprise.

GILBERT. I'm not sure which bags it is I'm supposed to take. Bert usually finds them…

FOREMAN (*pointing*). Over there. Get a move on.

GILBERT looks to where various trolleys full of bags are waiting for collection. There is a group of RAILWAY WORKERS near by – three white men leaning against a wall, smoking and drinking mugs of tea. GILBERT is tense as he walks over to the trolleys. The WORKERS fall silent as he begins to look through the bags, unsure as to which ones he should take.

GILBERT. Which ones are post?

WORKER 1. Did I hear someone speak?

The other WORKERS *laugh.* GILBERT *looks through the bags again.*

GILBERT. Can you help me please?

They are silent. Some are smirking, some are looking up at the ceiling as though they can't identify where the voice is coming from. GILBERT *moves to select another bag –*

WORKER 1. Look! A darkie's stealing from the railways!

GILBERT *puts the sack down and move to lifts another one –*

Oh, my God, what's the coon doing now?!

The other WORKERS *laugh.* GILBERT *tries another sack and the* WORKERS *make wincing noises.*

WORKER 2 (*sucking in his breath*). Ooh, you don't want to do that.

GILBERT. Can you please help me then?

WORKER 1. Speak English.

GILBERT. It is English I am speaking.

WORKER 1. What? Anyone understand what this coloured gentleman is after?

The WORKERS *laugh.*

GILBERT. Can you please tell me which ones I am to take and then I will go.

WORKER 3 (*moving forward*). All right. I'll tell you, if you answer something for me.

GILBERT. What?

WORKER 3. When are you going back to the jungle?

The WORKERS *laugh and nod with appreciation.* GILBERT *turns away and picks up another sack.*

(*Moving closer.*) Oi, darkie? You ain't answered me. When are you going back where you belong?

GILBERT (*looking him in the eye*). But I just got here, man, and I not fucked your wife yet.

Pause.

WORKER 3. What did you say? (*To the* WORKERS.) What did he say?

The other WORKERS *tense as they sense violence.*

(*To* GILBERT.) Fucking wog! What did you say?

GILBERT. Me? Nothing.

WORKER 3 *suddenly grabs* GILBERT *by the collar.* GILBERT *is taller than the man – he could easily punch him or push him to the ground – but he keeps his arms by his sides.*

WORKERS 1 *and* 2 (*to* WORKER 3). Hit him! Go on! Fucking hit him!

The FOREMAN *is hurrying towards them.*

FOREMAN. Oi!

WORKER 3 *lets go of* GILBERT, *pushing him as he does so.*

WORKER 3. Fucking uppity nigger! Needs teaching a fucking lesson!

FOREMAN (*to* GILBERT). You causing trouble?

WORKERS. Yes!

FOREMAN. Are you? Answer me!

GILBERT *struggles with his emotions but he knows what he has to do.*

GILBERT. I'm sorry. Sorry, man. I don't want to cause trouble.

FOREMAN. You better bloody not do, or you'll get your cards.

GILBERT. Sorry.

FOREMAN. You're all the fucking same.

GILBERT. I work hard. We all work hard.

WORKER 1. Yeah, right.

GILBERT. I'm sorry. Okay? No trouble.

WORKER 1. There's decent Englishmen that should be doing your job.

FOREMAN. That's enough! (*To* GILBERT.) That trolley. That trolley. Got it?

GILBERT. Yes, sir.

WORKER 3. I'll have to wash my fucking hands now I've touched him.

GILBERT *goes to the trolley.*

FOREMAN. Hurry up, and fuck off. (*To* WORKERS.) Tea break's over.

The WORKERS *gradually turn away and start to amble back to work.* GILBERT *begins to wheel the trolley away. He pauses for a moment, struggling with his anger. In his mind's eye,* ELWOOD *appears –*

ELWOOD. You'll be back, man. Tail between your legs. Why you fall for their lies again? Hey? Big-talk man?

ELWOOD *laughs.* GILBERT *comes back to reality, then goes on his way.*

Scene Four

*The evening of the same day. GILBERT's room. HORTENSE
has tidied and cleaned everything. The fire is on. There is a new
blanket on the armchair. The table is set for dinner. HORTENSE
is on her knees scrubbing the floor, a new basin beside her.
GILBERT enters, his face still clouded with anger and misery.
He sees her and stops still.*

GILBERT. Get up.

She pauses and stares up at him, surprised.

Get up.

HORTENSE. What's the matter…?

GILBERT. Get up off your knees.

HORTENSE. What are you talking about?

GILBERT. Get up. I will not see you on your knees. No wife of
mine will be on her knees in this country!

*HORTENSE is frightened now but she tries not to show it.
She stands up.*

HORTENSE. What are you shouting at me for? Is this how you
come home? I have been cleaning this place from top to
bottom. Look! I even buy you a blanket so you will be
warmer on your chair tonight! And now you think you can
shout at me!

GILBERT tries to steady his breathing.

You are a very rude man! You are a very ignorant…

GILBERT (*suddenly*). Shut up, woman!

*HORTENSE is silenced. She stands very still. After a moment,
she picks up the basin and carries it into the kitchen area.
Then she picks up a plate of food and takes it to the table.
She slams the plate down. GILBERT looks at it – a hard-
boiled egg, peeled, and some sliced potatoes. After a few
seconds, he looks at HORTENSE.*

What is this?

HORTENSE. I have also made your dinner.

GILBERT. What is this?

HORTENSE. It is egg, and chips. You tell me you like egg and chips.

GILBERT (*picking up a piece of potato*). This is not a chip. What is this?

HORTENSE. The woman down the stairs, she say you peel a potato and slice it up into fingers...

GILBERT. And cook it! You cook it! A chip is fried!

HORTENSE. Well, she didn't tell that to I!

> GILBERT *suddenly swipes the plate of food off the table.*
> HORTENSE *jumps back. She stares at the mess on the floor.*

What have you done? You oaf! You...

She is beyond words. She rushes towards the door and starts to take her coat off the hanger, but GILBERT *moves towards her.*

GILBERT. Where are you going?

HORTENSE. Out! I will not stay here...

GILBERT. No! No! No! *I* am going out!

He storms from the room and slams the door behind him. HORTENSE *stands very still for a few moments. Then, slowly, she starts to pick up the 'chips' from the floor. She takes them to the kitchen and puts them in the bin. She carries the basin of water into the living area and, kneeling down, begins to wash the floor again. She stops. She covers her face with her hands in despair.*

In HORTENSE's *mind's eye,* MISS JEWEL *enters. The sun is bright and hot.*

MISS JEWEL. Tell me de likkle rhyme you is learnin' at de school, me sprigadee.

HORTENSE. Not again.

MISS JEWEL. De Mr William rhyme. Come nah.

HORTENSE. I wandered lonely as a cloud
That floats on high o'er vales and hills
When all at once I saw a crowd
A host of golden daffodils.

MISS JEWEL *joins in on the word 'daffodils'.*

MISS JEWEL. Dem nuh have none ah dat daffodil in Jamaica.

HORTENSE. No, it is in England where the daffodils are.

MISS JEWEL. Ah. Hengland. Di mudda-land.

HORTENSE. You should learn to speak properly, Miss Jewel, like the King of England does.

MISS JEWEL *suddenly stands and clears her throat.*

MISS JEWEL. Ah walk under a cloud… and den me float over de ill… And me see Miss Hortense a look pon de daffodil dem.'

But then the sun fades. HORTENSE *is alone again. Tears begin to gather in her eyes and she wipes them away – she will not cry. She hears footsteps on the stairs and, quickly, she takes the basin to the sink and begins to empty the water away.* GILBERT *enters and closes the door behind him. He has a small parcel wrapped in newspaper in his hand. He watches* HORTENSE *for a moment. His anger has abated and his eyes are full of regret. He goes to the table, and puts the parcel down on it. He takes off his coat.*

GILBERT (*gently*). Hortense?

She doesn't respond or look at him.

Hortense, come and sit with me. I bring you a present. Come.

Slowly, HORTENSE *dries her hands and goes to the table. She sits down.* GILBERT *sits. He opens the parcel of newspaper. It contains fish and chips.*

These are chips. This is 'Fish and Chips'.

HORTENSE *glances at the food. It smells really good.*

Do you want a plate? Or do you want to eat it like the English do – straight from the paper.

HORTENSE. I will not eat from dirty paper.

GILBERT. No. You are quite right.

He puts some of the fish and chips on a plate for her, and hands her a fork. She takes the fork. He picks up his own fork and begins to eat. Slowly, HORTENSE *takes a chip and begins to eat too.*

So you went to the shops today.

You find everything you need?

HORTENSE. What is a darkie?

GILBERT *stops eating and looks at her.*

GILBERT. Someone call you that?

HORTENSE. Some boys shouted at I in the street. One of them... threw some rubbish. The woman down the stairs say not to take any notice but...

Pause. GILBERT *struggles to contain his emotions.*

GILBERT. It's not easy to live in this country, Hortense. I wish I could protect you from it all.

HORTENSE. I do not need protecting. I will not be staying in this vicinity. It is not a nice vicinity. As soon as I have a teaching job I will move to a better place.

GILBERT. Hortense...

HORTENSE. You find out where the department for education is?

GILBERT. I...

HORTENSE. No. Of course you didn't.

GILBERT. Don't get your hopes up nah, about a teaching job...

HORTENSE. I will not be staying in this place for long. Even if you do.

GILBERT *watches her with concern, as she eats her chips, beautifully.*

Scene Five

*The following afternoon. The living room. The room is empty.
From the hall, the sound of the front door opening and closing.
After a moment, BERNARD enters. He is wearing his
gaberdine, belted and fastened, and a trilby hat. He is holding
a small case. He stands just inside the doorway. He is pale, full
of emotion. He takes in the room.*

QUEENIE *enters from the kitchen. She is carrying a bundle of
washing which she has just taken off the washing line in the
garden. She suddenly sees BERNARD. She lets out a small cry
of shock –*

QUEENIE. Ah!

She drops the washing onto the floor.

BERNARD. Qu... Qu... Queenie, it's me.

He moves towards her but she backs away –

Sorry. Queenie, it's me.

*She leans over, putting her head downwards so as not to
faint. She starts to tremble.*

Sorry. I should have... I should have thought. Written ahead.
Perhaps you should sit down?

QUEENIE (*quietly*). Oh, my God. Oh, my God. Oh, my God.

*She makes it to a chair and sits, clinging onto the sides.
Tentatively, BERNARD crosses to the washing and begins to
pick it up from the floor. He puts it on the table. She stares at
him. After a moment, he tries to smile at her, but he is so
tense and upset that it looks more like a grimace. QUEENIE
struggles to steady her breathing.*

BERNARD. Where's Father?

Pause.

QUEENIE (*quietly*). Didn't you get my letters?

BERNARD. Not for a few... for a while.

QUEENIE. He died.

Pause.

BERNARD. Oh.

QUEENIE. I did write to you. Lots of times.

BERNARD. When… did he…?

QUEENIE. 1944.

> BERNARD *nods.* QUEENIE *watches him as he processes the information. She is still trembling.*

BERNARD. Shall I make you a cup of tea?

QUEENIE. Where have you been?

BERNARD. India. Mostly.

QUEENIE. Mostly?

BERNARD. Arrived back four months ago, but I had to go to Brighton for a while – check on Maxi's family. He had three children you see and…

QUEENIE. Who's Maxi?

BERNARD. Oh. George Maximillian. My friend. I'm sure I mentioned him in my letters. Didn't I? I was concerned about his family, you see? He has three…

QUEENIE. You've been back in England for four months?

BERNARD. Yes. Needed to make sure his wife was… coping. Didn't mean to stay so long.

> QUEENIE *nods. A snigger suddenly escapes for her mouth and she raises her hand to her face to stop it. But then she sniggers again and starts to laugh quietly. She covers her mouth with her hand and her shoulders shake. She is laughing but she is also crying.*

Queenie?

> *She pulls herself together quite suddenly.*

QUEENIE. I thought you were dead. Since the end of the war. I've thought you were dead.

BERNARD. I…

QUEENIE. Why didn't you write to me?

BERNARD. I…

QUEENIE. Yes?

BERNARD. I wasn't very well…

QUEENIE. Not well? What, did you lose the use of your hand? Couldn't write?

BERNARD. No… I…

QUEENIE. Your mind?

BERNARD *looks pained.*

Well, did you?!

BERNARD. I don't see that there's any … cause to shout.

QUEENIE. Don't you? Really? Don't you?!

There is a knock on the door.

GILBERT (*off*). Queenie!? Queenie, you all right!?

BERNARD (*astonished*). Who on earth is that?

BERNARD *strides to the door and opens it. On seeing* GILBERT *he starts and steps back.*

GILBERT. Who are you? Where's Queenie?

QUEENIE. It's all right, Gilbert.

BERNARD. Who are you?

GILBERT. I mus' see Queenie's all right.

QUEENIE *goes to the door.*

BERNARD. I beg your pardon?

QUEENIE. It's all right. (*To* BERNARD.) Gilbert's a lodger. This is my husband, Gilbert. This is Bernard.

GILBERT. Bernard? Man! You come back. Man! (*Holding out his hand.*) It's a pleasure to meet you, Mr…

BERNARD *slams the door in* GILBERT*'s face.*

QUEENIE. Don't do that!

BERNARD. What the devil do you mean – a lodger?

QUEENIE. He rents the room at the top. His wife's just come over to join him.

BERNARD. Are you telling me… you've been sharing this house with…?

QUEENIE. There's another one on the middle landing. Winston. They pay their rent. And it's a good job they do because it's the only way I've managed.

BERNARD. Tell them to leave.

QUEENIE. No!

BERNARD. Yes! I will not have… coolies living in my house!

QUEENIE. You don't walk in here and start telling me what to do!

BERNARD. This is my house! And I will not have them in here!

QUEENIE. You have no idea how hard I've worked to hold on to this place. No idea. I could have sold it. I almost did.

BERNARD. You could not have sold it. You would have had no right…

QUEENIE. Yes I would. I could have had you declared dead. But I didn't. And then you would have come back to nothing – no house, no Arthur, no me! Would that have been better? You idiot man!

Silence. BERNARD looks dazed. QUEENIE regrets her choice of words. She shakes her head – at a loss.

BERNARD (*quietly*). You could have chosen white lodgers.

Pause. QUEENIE goes into the kitchen. BERNARD can hear her getting a glass of water. BERNARD sits down. He stares at the room – at the things that have changed and the things that are the same. QUEENIE returns and leans against the wall near to the kitchen door.

Where's Father's chair?

QUEENIE. I moved it up to his room. It made me sad – looking at it empty.

BERNARD. How did he… die?

QUEENIE. He was shot. By some Yankee policemen.

BERNARD. What do you mean?

QUEENIE. It was an accident. Or they said it was. They covered the whole thing up. It was in Lincolnshire. He's buried up there. I managed to get a stone made.

Pause. BERNARD *struggles to take this in. His lower lip starts to tremble. She stares at him.*

You thought he was alive. All this time. But you didn't come back to him. When you could. I suppose you thought it was all right to let me go on looking after him.

Pause. BERNARD *is looking down.*

Did you lose your memory? That's what some people said. Bernard?

BERNARD. I don't want to talk about it. (*Appealingly.*) I'm back now, Queenie.

QUEENIE *nods. After a moment, she stands and picks up the washing. Then she moves towards the door.*

Where are you going?

QUEENIE. To make a bed up. You can have Arthur's room.

BERNARD. Can't I…? I rather thought I might sleep in our bed.

QUEENIE. All right then. I'll go in Arthur's room.

QUEENIE *leaves.*

Scene Six

*The following day. A miserable, bomb-damaged London street.
A crooked signpost points directions to different council offices
– 'Education Department', 'Planning Department'. GILBERT
is waiting. He looks worried. He is holding his hat in his hands,
turning it round and round. From time to time, someone (white)
hurries by.*

*After a moment, HORTENSE comes from the direction of the
offices. She is wearing her pristine white coat, hat and gloves.
She is holding her handbag and clutching some letters in her
hand. She reaches the street, hesitates for a moment, confused,
panicky, then begins to walk away. GILBERT sees her –*

GILBERT. Hortense!

> *He rushes towards her.* HORTENSE *changes direction and
> begins to walk another way.* GILBERT *goes after her.*

> How you get on? They say you have a job?

HORTENSE. Why are you here? I told you not to wait for me.

GILBERT. Wait! What they say?

HORTENSE. What business is it of yours? Leave me alone!
I don't want you here!

> HORTENSE *hurries purposefully away in another direction.*

GILBERT. You don't even know where you are!

> *A* MAN *(white) passes her, almost bumps into her.*

MAN. Watch where you're going!

> HORTENSE *stops very still and lowers her head.* GILBERT
> *approaches her carefully.*

GILBERT. Hortense? Hortense, no more cuss me. Tell me what
happen.

> *She is silent for a moment, trying to recover her composure.*

HORTENSE. They say I can't teach.

GILBERT. What they mean?

HORTENSE. They say I would have to train all over again. None of my qualifications count for anything. None of my letters of recommendation. They speak to I like I am a fool.

GILBERT. Man, that…

He shakes his head. A WOMAN *(white) passes by and stares at them. She tuts as she walks on.* GILBERT *waits for* HORTENSE *to speak.*

HORTENSE. I walk into a cupboard.

GILBERT *takes this in for a moment.*

GILBERT. Why you do that?

HORTENSE. Because I thought it was the door to leave by.

GILBERT. Oh.

HORTENSE. But it was a cupboard. The office women… they all laugh on me.

GILBERT. Oh dear. I see. And tell me, what was this cupboard like?

HORTENSE *looks at him – trying to read his intention.*

HORTENSE. There was a bucket and a mop.

GILBERT. Ah. Now that is a broom cupboard. I have walked into many broom cupboards. I walk into a broom cupboard, a stationery cupboard…

HORTENSE. This one had paper also.

GILBERT. Did it? Ah. Two functions. Now that is an interesting cupboard.

She stares at him. His eyes twinkle at her a little.

HORTENSE. Are you teasing me, Gilbert Joseph?

GILBERT. And what do you do when you come from the cupboard?

HORTENSE. I left the room.

GILBERT. You no say anything to the women who was laughing on you? You should have told them it was an interesting cupboard.

HORTENSE. It was a dirty cupboard.

GILBERT. Well then. Cha, you should tell them that you are used to clean cupboards where you come from.

HORTENSE. I am.

GILBERT. Oh, I don't doubt it, Miss Spitfire.

She looks at him sharply. He smiles, and for a moment it seems that she might smile back. But then her face falls back into despair.

Tell you what – you wan' see the King?

HORTENSE. What are you talking about…?

GILBERT. You ever been on a London bus?

HORTENSE. No.

GILBERT. We will take a ride on a red London bus. We will sit on the top deck. I will show you Buckingham Palace and the Houses of Parliament. Big Ben. Piccadilly Circus. All the fine sights. You like that?

She nods. But then her eyes fill with tears. She fights against them. GILBERT *moves to put his arm around her but then decides he'd better not.*

HORTENSE. I dreamed of coming to England.

GILBERT. And you are here. Not many people have their dream come true.

HORTENSE. But what am I to do now? If I can't teach.

GILBERT. Don't worry. Don't worry, Hortense. I can look after you.

HORTENSE. I don't need looking after!

Pause. GILBERT *thinks.*

GILBERT. Well then. What else can you do? Can you sew?

HORTENSE. Of course.

GILBERT. Is that 'of course' like you can cook? Or can you actually sew?

HORTENSE. I have been sewing since I was a child.

GILBERT. Good. Then I know where you might find some work. I talk to this boy I know.

HORTENSE. But I am a teacher.

GILBERT. Yes. And a teacher you will be, even when you are sewing. Look at me – I am a delivery driver, but one day... (*Stops.*)

HORTENSE. What?

GILBERT. One day... I will study the Law.

They look at one another. She realises that her own pain is reflected in his eyes. They are quiet for a moment.

HORTENSE. I can cook, Gilbert Joseph.

GILBERT. No you can't.

HORTENSE. My teacher say my sponge cake was the best outside a tea shop in England.

GILBERT. She tell you where this tea shop is? Because we must be sure not to go there.

She nods and suppresses a smile. He sees the smile playing on her lips and beams, delighted.

(*Holding out his hand to her.*) Come, madam. Your bus is awaiting.

He offers her his arm. She is tempted to take it – but doesn't. They leave.

Scene Seven

Late afternoon the same day. GILBERT*'s room. A key turns in
the lock and* BERNARD *enters. He switches on the light and
looks about him, frowning. He stares at the large trunk and
shakes his head. He sniffs. He goes over to the gas fire and
checks it's off. He goes over to the table and takes in the broken
chair leg. He looks angry.*

There are footsteps on the stairs and GILBERT *and*
HORTENSE *enter. On seeing* BERNARD *they stop still.*

GILBERT. What are you doing in here?

BERNARD. Looking round. There seems to be a smell of gas.
Hope you know how to use it correctly. You'll have the
whole house up in smoke.

GILBERT. This is our room. You shouldn't be in here.

BERNARD. I beg to differ. My house. My room.

GILBERT. I pay rent for this room.

HORTENSE. How you get in here?

BERNARD (*holding up the key*). I have keys to all the rooms.
Not that it's any of your concern.

GILBERT. Don't speak to her like that.

BERNARD. You're going to have to leave.

GILBERT. What?

BERNARD. Leave. As soon as possible. All of you. I'm selling
the house.

GILBERT. What are you talking about?

BERNARD. Do you speak English?

GILBERT. What Queenie say about this? Queenie the one who
rent us the room…

BERNARD. Do you mean Mrs Bligh?

GILBERT. She not say anything about selling the house.

BERNARD. This is my house and I wish you to leave. That's all you need to know.

GILBERT. I talk to Queenie first.

BERNARD. I know what's been going on. I've been talking to the neighbours. You took advantage of her good nature...

GILBERT. I did what?

BERNARD. Met your sort out east. But now I'm back and we intend to live respectably again. It's what I fought a war for. (*Moving towards the door.*) I want you out by the end of the week.

GILBERT. I fought in the war too. I fought the same war as you. Now I just looking for a decent life.

BERNARD. Decent? Decent? You call this decent? Look at what you've done to the place. It's a disgrace!

GILBERT *is shocked into silence.*

HORTENSE. We do our best to make it nice...

BERNARD. This used to be Mother's sewing room. It used to be spotless.

HORTENSE. What can we do when the furniture is all broken and the fire is not working right and...

BERNARD. Well, you could try harder.

GILBERT *suddenly lunges at* BERNARD, *pushing him back against the table.*

GILBERT. Get out!

HORTENSE. Gilbert!

GILBERT. Get out of my room!

BERNARD *pushes him back.*

BERNARD. No! It's you who must get out!

They tussle.

HORTENSE. Stop! Stop!

BERNARD. I'll call the police! I'll call the police!

HORTENSE. Gilbert!

GILBERT. You don't speak to my wife like that!

BERNARD. Get... off... me!

Suddenly QUEENIE *enters. She is flushed, panting. She looks as though she's in pain. She clings on to the door for support.*

QUEENIE. What the bloody hell is going on?

GILBERT *lets go of* BERNARD.

BERNARD. I was just telling these... these *people* that they have to leave.

GILBERT. He come in here without asking. He say you selling the house. This true?

BERNARD. I'll thank you to address your questions to me!

QUEENIE. Oh, shut up, Bernard! Shut up and calm down.

BERNARD *is stunned. He stares at her, his mouth gaping.*

GILBERT (*smirking*). You gonna listen to your wife nah, man?

BERNARD (*turning on him*). You will leave this house tonight. I will not have wogs living in my house.

GILBERT *launches himself at* BERNARD *again.* BERNARD *puts his fists up and tries to fend him off.*

HORTENSE. No! Gilbert!

QUEENIE. Stop it!

GILBERT. You ras clot!

BERNARD. Savages! Savages!

QUEENIE *suddenly cries out – a long drawn-out cry of agony. The men back off each other and stare at her.*

Queenie?

QUEENIE *is panting and groaning.*

GILBERT (*moving towards her*). What's wrong, Queenie?

BERNARD. Don't touch her!

GILBERT. I just trying to…

QUEENIE *lets out another dreadful cry.*

BERNARD (*moving towards her*). Queenie?

QUEENIE. No! Leave me alone.

BERNARD. But what's the matter?

QUEENIE. Don't touch me! Don't touch me!

She leans against the wall, panting.

Go away.

BERNARD. But what's the matter?

QUEENIE. Hortense, you stay.

GILBERT *glances at* HORTENSE. *She looks horrified.*

GILBERT. You want Hortense to stay with you?

HORTENSE. What…?

QUEENIE. Please. Please.

BERNARD. This is ludicrous. I will stay with you, Queenie…

QUEENIE. No! Just Hortense. Just Hortense.

GILBERT *realises what's happening.*

GILBERT. Oh, Lord. I think this a woman thing. Hortense, I will stay close by.

HORTENSE. What? No.

QUEENIE *is overcome by another contraction. She groans and howls in agony.*

GILBERT. Oh, man. (*To* BERNARD.) You should leave, man.

BERNARD. Don't tell me what to do!

GILBERT. I'll be outside, Hortense.

HORTENSE. Wait.

GILBERT *leaves*.

BERNARD. Queenie, I am fetching a doctor.

QUEENIE (*through the pain*). No!

BERNARD. But...

QUEENIE. I don't need one, Bernard. I promise you. I just need to...

She groans again.

BERNARD. Queenie?

QUEENIE. Jesus Christ! Just go, Bernard! Just bloody go!

BERNARD, *bewildered and afraid, leaves the room.*

(*To* HORTENSE.) Shut the door.

HORTENSE *does so, reluctantly.*

Put something in front of it.

HORTENSE. But... You want me to shut him out?

QUEENIE *doesn't reply – she is panting.* HORTENSE *pushes the trunk in front of the door.*

QUEENIE. Boil some water.

HORTENSE (*hesitating*). You want a cup of tea?

But QUEENIE *isn't listening.* HORTENSE *goes into the kitchen area and puts the kettle on.* QUEENIE *grabs a blanket off the bed and lays it on the floor.*

QUEENIE (*quietly*). God. Oh, God.

She reaches under her skirt and pulls her knickers off. Then she takes her blouse off to reveal the binding around her tummy. She starts to undo it. HORTENSE *has returned and is staring at her.*

Help me.

HORTENSE. Mrs Bligh – are you with child?

QUEENIE. Not for much longer, I'm not. It's coming, Hortense.

QUEENIE *tosses the binding aside.*

HORTENSE. Oh, no. No. You must have a doctor. You must go to the hospital...

QUEENIE. No time. There's no time. It's been coming since this morning.

QUEENIE *lies down on the blanket.*

I need you to look.

HORTENSE. What? I don't know anything about...

QUEENIE. Yes, you do.

HORTENSE. I don't. I can't.

QUEENIE. Think of *Gone with the Wind*. Oh Jesus Christ!

QUEENIE *has another contraction.*

Look! Oh, please, Hortense.

HORTENSE *kneels down on the floor and looks under* QUEENIE*'s skirt.*

HORTENSE. Can you open your legs a little wider, please, Mrs Bligh?

QUEENIE (*doing so*). Oh, for Christ's sake, call me Queenie!

HORTENSE *looks. She looks away again.*

HORTENSE. Oh, my.

QUEENIE. Is it there?

HORTENSE. Yes. Your baby is definitely coming, Mrs Bligh.

QUEENIE. Is it? Did you see the head?

HORTENSE. Yes.

QUEENIE. Oh!

HORTENSE. I think perhaps you need to push, Mrs Bligh.

QUEENIE. Yes. Yes.

With the next contraction QUEENIE *bears down. Her groans of agony alarm* BERNARD, *who knocks on the door.*

BERNARD (*off*). Queenie! What's going on?

HORTENSE (*calling*). Just a woman's matter! No worry!

QUEENIE *stops pushing and tries to breathe.* HORTENSE *looks under her skirt again.*

The head is out.

QUEENIE. Is it? Is it?

HORTENSE. Yes. You must push again. Push again.

QUEENIE. You'll have to catch it.

HORTENSE. Don't worry. Push again now.

QUEENIE *pushes with the next contraction.* HORTENSE *guides the baby out.*

Oh, my. Oh, my. Your baby is here.

BERNARD (*off*). Queenie!

HORTENSE. It's here. I have it.

QUEENIE. Let me see.

HORTENSE. It's still attached.

QUEENIE. Let me see.

HORTENSE *shows her the baby. The baby starts to cry.*

It's all right. Oh, it's all right little one. It's a boy, isn't it? A lovely perfect boy.

It's all right.

QUEENIE *takes the baby from* HORTENSE. *There are splatters of blood on* HORTENSE's *white clothes. As the baby cries, his colour becomes more and more apparent.* HORTENSE *stares at him.*

Oh, look at him. Look, Hortense.

HORTENSE. Mrs Bligh... your baby is... I think your baby is black.

QUEENIE (*to baby*). Oh, you're beautiful. My beautiful boy.

HORTENSE. Can you hear me, Mrs Bligh? Your baby is black. How come your baby is...?

GILBERT (*off*). Hortense? What 'appening in there? Let me in!

BERNARD (*off*). Get away from that door. Stand away from me.

HORTENSE*'s expression has changed. Is this* GILBERT*'s child? She moves the trunk aside and opens the door. She steps to one side.* BERNARD *strides in and, seeing* QUEENIE *and the baby, stops in his tracks.* GILBERT *follows him in and stops too.* GILBERT *stares at the baby and then at* HORTENSE. HORTENSE *looks away.*

GILBERT. But...

BERNARD (*to* GILBERT). You. You!

BERNARD *is about to attack* GILBERT –

QUEENIE. It's not his! He's not his. Gilbert has nothing to do with him. I swear it on his life. I swear.

BERNARD *is very still for a moment, then he rushes from the room. His footsteps can be heard thundering down the stairs.* GILBERT *and* HORTENSE *stare at* QUEENIE *and her baby.*

Scene Eight

Two hours later. QUEENIE*'s bedroom.* QUEENIE *carries her swaddled baby to the window and looks out into the darkness.*

She stares down at her sleeping baby. She lowers her head to his and breathes him in.

In QUEENIE*'s mind's eye,* MICHAEL *appears behind her, very close to her. She feels his presence, remembering –*

MICHAEL (*quietly, like a bedtime story*). We have a bird in Jamaica – a hummingbird. It is very small but beautiful – blue, green, purple, red in its tiny feathered body. And when it flies, its wings flicker so fast your eye cannot see them. One time in this city, when the bombs had fallen, everywhere I look is devastation. But then you know what I see?

QUEENIE. What?

MICHAEL. A hummingbird. In the middle of the rubble and the bricks, a hummingbird. I thought my eyes was playing tricks on me – a madness from the flying and the fight. But not only I saw it. A hummingbird on a London street. I watched that bird like I see an old friend. It looked dowdier in the grey British light – no sun to sparkle it up. But there it was, so far from home. And happy, to sample the nectar of the English flowers.

They are entwined now, QUEENIE *leaning back into* MICHAEL, *his breath against her cheek.*

QUEENIE. This is our son, Michael. We made him. This is our beautiful boy.

Darkness descends. MICHAEL *leaves.* QUEENIE *places the baby in the drawer. She tucks him in. Then she gets into bed and sleeps.*

Time passes. The middle of the night. QUEENIE *is sleeping – exhausted. The baby begins to cry, quietly and sporadically. After a few moments, the door opens and* BERNARD *comes in. He stands in the doorway, allowing his eyes to adjust to the near-darkness. Then he creeps across to the drawer. He squats down and looks at the baby. He reaches down and touches his cheek, gently –*

BERNARD. Hush now.

The baby stops crying. BERNARD *picks him up.*

There, there.

He stands, and settles the baby into the crook of his arm. The baby sucks on his finger. BERNARD *rocks him.*

(*Singing quietly.*) Hush, here comes the Dream Man. Hush, here comes the Dream Man. Now you children run up the stairs, put on your nighties and say your prayers…

QUEENIE *has awoken. She sits up slightly and stares at* BERNARD – *instantly alert, anxious.*

Then ride with Mr Dream Man, till daylight comes again…

He sees QUEENIE *watching him. He stares at her for a few moments, then smiles, sadly.*

He was crying. (*Looking down at the baby.*) Sweet little fellow.

Pause.

QUEENIE. I'm sorry.

His father was an RAF man. A brave man. I was so lonely. Especially after Arthur went. I thought you were gone. I was so lonely.

Pause.

BERNARD. I should have been a better husband to you, Queenie. I meant to be. I did want to come home. I missed you.

QUEENIE (*carefully*). What happened out there?

BERNARD *shakes his head slightly.*

I know you went to prison.

BERNARD. Who told you that?

QUEENIE. The RAF. When I tried to find you.

BERNARD. No business telling you that.

QUEENIE. I wanted to know. I want to understand. Bernard?

Pause.

BERNARD. You asked me if I lost my mind – in a way… I think I did. After Maxi… After Calcutta.

QUEENIE. What happened?

Pause. BERNARD *is staring down at the baby, clutching the baby's tiny hand.*

BERNARD. They sent us in to break up the riots. Only they weren't riots. It was a bloodbath. Slaughter. Hindu against Muslim against Sikh. Slaughtering each other. Brown bodies everywhere. Guts pulled forth. Vultures… feeding off the dead. Ordered to break up a fight. Maxi went in first – he was like that – always the first. They set fire to him.

QUEENIE. No.

BERNARD. I tried to help him. Dropped my weapon. One of the bastards stole it.

QUEENIE. You were put in prison for that?

BERNARD. They put me in with the natives, Queenie. With the thieves. With the murderers. Like I was no better.

QUEENIE. Bernard.

Pause.

BERNARD. He was my only friend out there. The only one who didn't think I was a… joke.

Called me 'Pop' – that bit older, you see? Never had a nickname before. He saw me through.

BERNARD *has tears on his face.*

QUEENIE. I'm so sorry.

BERNARD. Think I lost my mind. Did some things I'm ashamed of. Dreadful things. Repulsive things. Thought I had VD for a while. Turned out to be malaria. Don't remember much about that.

QUEENIE. Why didn't you write to me? I would have done anything I could to help you.

He looks at her with gratitude and affection.

BERNARD. Felt I didn't deserve you. Didn't want to come home like Father did. Home from the war – lifted out of the back of a truck, dumped on the doorstep, gibbering. Neighbours watching. Didn't want that.

Don't know what's happening, Queenie.

QUEENIE. Bernard...

The baby is starting to cry again.

BERNARD. I'm afraid my finger won't do any more.

He takes the baby to QUEENIE *and hands him to her, gently.*

I'm sorry.

BERNARD *leaves.*

Scene Nine

Four days later. Afternoon. The living room. QUEENIE *is sitting with the baby on her lap. She is dressing him.*

QUEENIE. That's it. Make you smart.

She hears the front door open and close and quiet laughter in the hall. Hurriedly, she puts the baby in his drawer, rushes to the door and opens it.

Gilbert. Hortense. Will you come in for a moment?

GILBERT (*off*). Sorry, Queenie. We only come back to change. We going out with some of the...

QUEENIE. Please. Just for a moment.

GILBERT *and* HORTENSE *enter reluctantly.* QUEENIE *closes the door behind them.*

GILBERT. It good to see you up and about.

QUEENIE *takes some money from the table and holds it out to* GILBERT.

QUEENIE. I wanted to give you this. For the cleaning. For your dress, Hortense.

HORTENSE. Oh, there's no need, Mrs Bligh.

QUEENIE. There is. And it's Queenie.

GILBERT *takes the money.*

GILBERT. Thank you.

QUEENIE. Bernard tells me you're moving out.

GILBERT. Yes. End of the week.

QUEENIE. Where will you go?

GILBERT. Finsbury Park. Winston have a bit of luck. He inherit some money from an uncle back home. He bought a bombed-out place in Finsbury Park. It need a lot of work but...

HORTENSE. It is going to be a fine house. We will make it very fine.

QUEENIE. Good. That's good. I'm sure it will be.

Sit down.

GILBERT. No. Thank you. We...

QUEENIE. I'll make tea. And I've got biscuits.

GILBERT. Where's your husband?

QUEENIE. Oh, don't worry about him. He's doing some work in the garden. Arthur's veg patch. Sit down. You'll want to see the baby.

HORTENSE *and* GILBERT *glance at each other and then reluctantly perch on the edge of the sofa.* QUEENIE *fetches the baby from the drawer.*

Here he is. He's a bit less of a fright now.

She hands him to HORTENSE, *who doesn't really feel confident to take him.*

Let me help you. Just bend your arm a bit. No... Have you never held a baby before?

HORTENSE. Of course.

GILBERT *helps* HORTENSE *to find the right position.*

QUEENIE. That's it.

He's a lovely boy. Good as gold. No bother.

HORTENSE (*to baby*). Hello. (*Moving to hand him back.*) He's very sweet.

QUEENIE. Oh, no, no – you keep him. He likes you. That's his happy noise.

GILBERT. You have a name for him?

QUEENIE. Michael.

HORTENSE *flinches with surprise.*

Oops – careful.

HORTENSE. Michael?

QUEENIE. Do you like it?

HORTENSE. Michael was the name of someone very dear to me. My cousin. It is a favourite name of mine.

QUEENIE. I'm glad.

They look at each other for a moment. From the kitchen the back door is heard opening and closing.

GILBERT. That your husband?

QUEENIE. Don't worry about him.

GILBERT (*standing*). We should go, Hortense.

QUEENIE. No! No.

There is the sound of water running in the kitchen.

GILBERT. I don't want him to find us here.

QUEENIE. But...

HORTENSE *holds out the baby to her.*

GILBERT. Thank you. Sorry about the tea...

QUEENIE (*suddenly*). Will you take him?

HORTENSE *looks at her, confused.*

HORTENSE. But… I already have him, Mrs…

QUEENIE. No. I mean… will you take him with you – when you leave? When you move?

Take him and look after him.

Silence.

GILBERT. What are you saying?

QUEENIE *suddenly drops to her knees in front of them.*

QUEENIE. Please. I trust you. I know you. You're good people.

HORTENSE. No, Mrs Bligh…

QUEENIE. Please. Oh please. I'm begging you. For his sake. Take him and look after him. Please. Please.

BERNARD *appears in the doorway to the kitchen.*

BERNARD. Queenie. What in God's name are you doing?

QUEENIE *stares at the floor, unable to reply.*

That's your child. What are you thinking? You're his mother…

QUEENIE. But I can't look after him.

BERNARD. Why? Why ever not?

QUEENIE. How can I? I don't even know how to comb his hair.

BERNARD. But that's ridiculous. We would work something out. You are not giving your child away to these people.

QUEENIE. But…

BERNARD. *We'll* bring him up. Together.

QUEENIE. What?

BERNARD. We'll say he's adopted. It's quite simple.

QUEENIE. Oh, Bernard... No...

BERNARD. An orphan...

QUEENIE. No...

BERNARD. There's been a war. All sorts of things have happened...

QUEENIE. No! It wouldn't work. I know it wouldn't. You wouldn't be able to bear it...

BERNARD. Yes, I would. If I have to.

QUEENIE. No. You might think you can do it now – he's little now. It's easy. He's sweet. But he's going to grow up into a... a big, strapping coloured lad. And people will snigger at you in the street and ask you awkward questions...

BERNARD. We'll tell them he's adopted.

QUEENIE. All those proper, decent neighbours in the suburbs who'll turn their backs on us. Are you going to punch the other dads 'cause the kids call him names? Are you going to be proud of him? Glad that he's your son?

Pause. BERNARD *can't answer.*

I've thought about nothing else. And you know what? I don't think *I've* got the guts for it. I thought I would have... I should have, but I haven't. And I'm his mother.

(*To* GILBERT *and* HORTENSE.) I'd have to give him to an orphanage.

BERNARD. Queenie...

QUEENIE. And they don't want the coloured ones.

BERNARD. We should talk about this in private.

QUEENIE. They're sending all the half-caste babies to America. America, Gilbert – can you imagine? They'd treat him like dirt. They'd send him up the back in the picture hall.

GILBERT. Queenie...

QUEENIE (*crying*). You'd love him. I know you would...

BERNARD. Queenie, this is not the solution.

QUEENIE. And you could write to me. And you could tell him that I loved him. So much. So much.

She begins to sob.

GILBERT (*lifting her up*). Queenie. Come, nah.

BERNARD. Get your filthy black hands off my wife!

Silence.

GILBERT. You know what your trouble is, man?

BERNARD. I'm not interested in your opinion.

GILBERT. Your white skin. You think it give you the right to lord it over a black man. But you know what it make you? White. That is all, man. White. No better, no worse than me. We both just finish fighting a war for a better world we want to see. But still, after all we suffer together, you wan' tell me that I am worthless and you are not. Am I to be the servant and you the master for all time? Because you white? No. Stop this, man. We can work together, Mr Bligh. We want the same thing – a decent home, some work, some self-respect, some love. We can work together. You no see? Man, we must. Or we just go on fighting each other to the end. Fighting and fighting. And what then? What then?

Pause. HORTENSE *is staring at* GILBERT, *full of pride.*

BERNARD. I'm sorry... (*Pause.*) but I simply can't understand a single word you're saying.

Pause.

GILBERT. Come, Hortense.

HORTENSE *hands the baby back to* QUEENIE.

QUEENIE. What? No...

GILBERT *takes* HORTENSE'*s hand and they walk towards the door.*

No! Gilbert!

GILBERT *and* HORTENSE *leave.* QUEENIE *sits down on the sofa with Michael and sobs.*

Scene Ten

GILBERT*'s room.* GILBERT *and* HORTENSE *enter.* GILBERT *closes the door behind them. Silence.*

HORTENSE. That just happen?

This is not what I was expecting in England.

GILBERT *is deep in thought – frowning, conflicted.*

That poor little child.

GILBERT. A child belong with its mother. Doesn't it?

HORTENSE *considers this.*

HORTENSE. My mother gave me away. Because of my skin.
She thought there was the chance of a golden life for I.
I hardly remember her – a flapping black skirt... bare black
feet skipping over stones. But I remember the people who
love me. Miss Jewel. Michael.

GILBERT. So this Michael... he really was your cousin?

HORTENSE. Yes. Michael Roberts was my cousin.

*They are quiet for a moment – each lost in their own
thoughts.*

GILBERT. I don't want to leave that little coloured baby alone
in this country. This country full of people like Mr Bligh.

HORTENSE. I know.

GILBERT. What sort of chance will he have? What sort of life?
Always different. Always despised. He will grow up feeling
he is inferior. I can't have that. I can't allow that.

HORTENSE (*quietly*). No.

*She watches him as he struggles to work out the right thing
to do.*

I was proud of you, Gilbert Joseph. The way you spoke to
Mr Bligh. The words you said. Your dignity. You will be an
excellent lawyer.

*He is surprised, moved. She goes to him, reaches out and
touches his face, gently, tracing its lines. Then she kisses him.*

He kisses her back. They stop, and stare into each other's eyes. She leans against him and he puts his arm around her – carefully.

GILBERT. Oh, Hortense.

She makes a decision.

HORTENSE. It's very cold this evening.

GILBERT. It always cold.

HORTENSE *goes to the armchair. She takes the blanket from it and brings it over to the bed.* GILBERT*'s heart skips a beat. He watches her as she spreads it on the bed. He smiles at her and she smiles back. She stops still –*

HORTENSE. You wan' us to take the child, Gilbert?

Scene Eleven

The stage is empty but for QUEENIE. *She is walking up and down with the baby in her arms. Waiting.*

1948. December 15th. 11.28 a.m.

QUEENIE *stops.*

QUEENIE (*to audience*). There are some words that once spoken will split the world in two.

GILBERT *and* HORTENSE *enter and go to her.*

Will you take my son?

GILBERT. We cannot know for certain what his future will be. But we do know that we will be proud of him.

HORTENSE. And he will be loved.

QUEENIE *hands the baby to* HORTENSE. *Behind them,* BERNARD *enters and comes to stand close by, watching.*

HORTENSE *hands the baby to* GILBERT.

ARTHUR *enters. He is followed by all the other characters of the play* – ELWOOD, DOROTHY, MISS JEWEL, QUEENIE*'s parents, etc. They watch as* GILBERT *hands the baby to* BERNARD. BERNARD *stares down at the baby for a few moments, and then hands him to* QUEENIE.

MICHAEL *enters. He is carrying a basket. He places the basket on the ground in front of* QUEENIE, GILBERT, HORTENSE *and* BERNARD.

QUEENIE *kisses the baby's head. Then, slowly, she places him carefully into the basket.*

The lights start to fade. There is a sense of water around the basket. The basket is floating on the water, and the characters watch it from the land. The lights fade down until there is only a spotlight on this baby – made by all of us – floating into an uncertain world.

End.

www.nickhernbooks.co.uk

facebook.com/nickhernbooks

twitter.com/nickhernbooks